USE THE CF
TO GROW
YOUR B2B BUSINESS

A PROVEN STRATEGY FOR ENDURING COMPETITIVE ADVANTAGE AND BUSINESS GROWTH, ESPECIALLY IN TIMES OF CRISIS OR RECESSION

JOHN B. HAYES

Act now to use the credit crisis to grow your business and gain a long-term competitive advantage.

To obtain the most information from this book with the shortest investment of time, read Chapters 1, 2, and 13, which should take no more than 30 minutes of your time. This may be the most valuable 30 minutes that you spend this year.

Chapter 1: *Introduction - background and need for the strategy*

Chapter 2: *Executive Summary - outlines the strategy*

Chapter 13: *Roadmap - decision tree for funding the strategy*

USING THE CREDIT CRISIS TO GROW YOUR B2B BUSINESS

A Proven Strategy for Enduring Competitive Advantage and Business Growth, Especially in Times of Crisis or Recession

Published by:
Plain Talk Press
Atlanta, Georgia
www.plaintalkpress.net

Copyright © 2008 by Plain Talk Press
ISBN: 978-0-9727942-1-3
Library of Congress Control Number: 2008921510
Manufactured in the United States of America

1.0

ABOUT THE AUTHOR

John Hayes has been designing and building successful financial applications on Intel processors with Microsoft software longer than anyone. In 1975, John Hayes organized the team that created Altair Accounting, renamed in 1978 as Peachtree Accounting Software, the first mass-adopted financial application for personal computers. Since that time Hayes has created a number of other widely-adopted software products and systems that serve millions of business users. Trained as a systems engineer and a lawyer, Hayes has represented thousands of individual businesses and has developed a unique insight into the financial systems by which businesses operate. Hayes's most recent effort has been to create the FTRANS® payment system that provides B2B sellers the opportunity to outsource trade credit risk, business processes, and funding (just as retailers outsource consumer credit in accepting a credit card for payment) while not disrupting the traditional trade credit benefits that business buyers require.

As part of a long-term effort to make financial information more accessible to business owners, Hayes has created the *Capital Flow Model*™ that provides a visual look at the flow of capital in a business. Hayes says, "The Capital Flow Model is a tool that gives a visual representation of the critical flow of capital in the business. Having a graphical view of the relationship of inputs and outputs of capital helps people visualize important dynamics in a business, frequently easier than examining debits and credits on financial statements." The Capital Flow Model is used in this book both to analyze the capital flow relationships in a business and to demonstrate how to apply the strategy advocated by this book.

ACKNOWLEDGEMENTS

The author acknowledges and thanks the team members of FTRANS Corp., the business clients of FTRANS, the team members of The CIT Group, the bank partners of FTRANS, especially the banks of the Synovus Financial Corporation and Darby Bank & Trust, and the hundreds of other bankers, lawyers, accountants, bank association professionals, and commercial finance professionals who, through intense discussions and actual transactions, have helped the author understand the flows of capital in business enterprises that form the basis of this book. The author also thanks the more than one thousand business clients over the past 30 years whose successes and failures have contributed to the author's understanding and appreciation of the interplay between the legal and financial frameworks of businesses. The author also thanks the millions of users of Peachtree Accounting Software over the past 30 years, especially those in the first few years when all personal computer software was a challenge for users, for creating something in which he takes an immense sense of pride – a large and largely satisfied user base. Finally, the author thanks his wife, Gail, and their two children, Sarah and Katie, who have each dedicated their lives to improving the lives of others, for being the people they are.

DEDICATION

This book is dedicated to the millions of owners of small and middle-size businesses in the United States who, against great odds, have created and sustained the most vibrant economy the world has ever seen.

TABLE OF CONTENTS

APPENDICES

INTRODUCTION: WHY THIS BOOK WAS WRITTEN

Inform business owners of all sizes on how to use a simple and proven strategy to grow their businesses, especially in this time of credit contraction, and create an enduring competitive advantage. The strategy described works for almost all businesses that sell to other businesses or to governments (B2B sellers).

CRISIS BRINGS OPPORTUNITY.

Never has this statement been more correct than it is today for the vast majority of American businesses. A world credit crisis began in mid-2007, precipitated by the meltdown in subprime mortgage lending in the United States and has now spread to other credit markets worldwide. This credit crisis has caused the global credit markets to contract and is causing banks in the United States to become much more restrictive in their lending.

The result is a crisis in access to credit – only larger and more credit-worthy borrowers will continue to have the same access to credit that most businesses have enjoyed for the past ten years. Smaller and middle-sized business enterprises will feel the credit crisis most directly, as they always do.

But, in this credit crisis lays a significant opportunity, the opportunity for businesses that sell to other businesses (B2B sellers) *to grow their businesses by granting to their buyers more credit on more flexible terms*. At the same time sellers are growing their businesses, they are building relationships with buyers that can be an enduring competitive advantage for years to come.

The opportunity for growing a business by granting more credit to customers is not new; it has existed for thousands of years. But, the opportunity to use this strategy in the business to business (B2B) market has become highly magnified in recent months as a result of the current credit crisis. Business owners that understand the role of trade credit in funding their own business and in funding the businesses of their customers can take advantage of this simple strategy to grow and profit greatly from this current credit crisis.

Another title for this book could have been *Use Your Customers' Greatest Need to Grow Your Business.* While that statement is true (and will continue to be true after the current credit crisis abates), this current crisis is shining a spotlight on the credit needs of customers, and B2B sellers can take advantage of this need in the short term. The advantage of this strategy does not diminish in the long term – granting more credit to business customers will be as important a strategy in 2028 as it is in 2008. The strategy has been important for thousands of years and will continue to be important for a long time.

The simple fact is that more businesses in America depend on trade credit funded by their vendors (their accounts payable) as their largest source of capital, more than bank loans and owners equity. The "give more trade credit" strategy advocated by this book to take advantage of this fact, in light of the current credit crisis, is also simple:

> More American businesses already depend on trade credit from their vendors as their largest source of capital, more than bank loans and owners equity. The vendor that can provide more business credit during a credit crisis will gain more current business and will create an enduring loyalty, perhaps even dependence, on the part of their buyers.

During the nearly 40 years that I have been working with businesses, large and small, as an entrepreneur, a lawyer, and as a systems engineer building business software and systems, I have been given the opportunity to observe many aspects of these clients. One of my observations is that a surprising number of business owners and managers, even very successful ones, do not have a complete understanding of the financial underpinnings of their business. They may be using quality accounting software, such as Peachtree Accounting, QuickBooks, or Microsoft Dynamics, to keep their books. They may understand generally how to read financial statements and have a basic understanding of the role of capital in operating and growing their businesses. But, a significant number of business owners and managers do not fully understand the role their business plays in funding their customers and the cost to their own business in playing that role.

This book was written to explain not just that role, but how to use the role of being a provider of capital to customers to grow your business and create enduring loyalty, especially in this time of a crisis in the availability of credit.

This book uses two tools to analyze the financial situation of businesses and explain the "give more trade credit" strategy. These tools are discussed throughout this book as they are applied. A summary of each tool is found in Appendix C. The two tools are:

The **Capital Flow Model** provides a graphical view of the flow of capital in a business and facilitates a rapid comprehension of the relationship of capital sources and uses.

The **Three Cs of Lending**, a traditional way for bankers to evaluate loan prospects, provides a framework for understanding how bankers view a variety of lending situations, including working capital loans and the current subprime mortgage meltdown. Understanding the Three Cs will help you understand how bankers perceive your business and that of your customers.

EXECUTIVE SUMMARY

Summary of the strategy in three pages.

The "give more trade credit" strategy presented by this book is summarized in the following seven statements. References are provided for more detailed explanations of each point. A road map is provided in Chapter 13 for pursuing sources of capital to execute this strategy.

The credit extended by business vendors (sellers) to their business customers (buyers) is the largest source of capital for more businesses in the United States than any other source, including bank loans or investments and loans by owners.

Accounts payable is such a critical source of capital that buyers will frequently select sellers based on their ability or willingness to extend credit. Wal-Mart, Home Depot, Federated, Target, and hundreds of other large buyers simply require their vendors to provide 45 days, 60 days, or longer terms for payment. See Chapters 3 and 4.

Trade credit has been an important part of commerce for thousands of years.

The modern banking system was created largely to facilitate commerce and trade credit, but in recent years banks have backed away from playing a significant role in funding trade credit. The result is that vendor-provided capital is more critical for most buyers. See Chapters 4 and 5.

The current credit crisis will create financial stress for many of your business customers; helping to reduce that stress will enable you to sell more now and create enduring loyalty.

The current credit crisis is causing banks to be more conservative in their lending, restricting both the amount of capital available and the number of business borrowers that will qualify for credit. This contraction in credit availability also impacts the appetite of equity investors and their ability to invest. This credit crisis may also cause some of your competitors (the ones that have not implemented the strategy outlined in this book) to limit the credit they give to their customers. The result is that less capital is available for many of your customers, which will create stress on their businesses. By offering more trade credit and longer payment terms to your business customers, you can help relieve some of this stress, which can result in their buying more from you and becoming more dependent on you for funding their business. See Chapters 6 and 7.

The traditional way to increase funding to customers (increasing your accounts receivable, which is a "use of capital") requires increasing the capital available to you, the seller.

The traditional way for a business to increase the funding provided to its customers (the "output" side of the flow of funds) is to increase the capital available from the following "input" sources: (1) increase your funding from vendors – your accounts payable, (2) increase borrowing from banks or other sources (including receivables financing), or (3) increase the equity in the business. While these traditional sources of capital are being constricted by the credit crisis, they have not been closed completely and may offer alternatives, especially increasing funding from vendors (your accounts payable). See Chapter 9.

A new method of outsourcing trade credit is now available that allows increasing the funding to customers while reducing the capital required.

This seemingly contradictory method has already been accomplished by almost all retailers and other B2C (business to consumer) sellers through the use of the bank credit card system. It is now available for B2B (business to business) sellers through a new method of outsourcing trade credit. See Chapter 10. [Author's disclaimer: this method was developed by FTRANS, a company I founded and I have a financial stake in its success.]

Using the accounts receivable of your company and that of a target acquisition can help fund growth through acquisitions.

This simple strategy is frequently used in large merger and acquisition transactions; it can be used by smaller companies as well, provided they know how to replace the accounts receivables with cash. Two case studies are provided. See Chapter 11.

Several case studies are provided that illustrate real-world examples of this strategy being deployed.

Case studies from wholesale distribution, manufacturing, staffing, and services are provides to help illustrate the application of the strategy. See Chapter 12.

THE CAPITAL FLOW MODEL

The Capital Flow Model: A systems engineering view of the flow of funds in a business with particular emphasis on sources and uses of capital.

Most of us learned to think about the flow of capital in a business through the lens of traditional financial statements, and usually only a subset of the important financial statements – the Income Statement (also called the Statement of Profit and Loss) and the Balance Sheet (also called the Statement of Financial Position). Whether we studied these two financial statements in formal courses in accounting or finance, or learned them on the job, the result is similar. We think about the financial affairs of business today through a lens that was initially constructed about 125 years ago in a traditional presentation of financial statements that classifies balance sheet transactions into assets, liabilities, or equity. This lens was developed in the late 1800s to facilitate the comparison of companies, primarily railroads that were raising capital in the public markets. Through this lens we are viewing a system of accounting developed more than 600 years ago – double-entry accounting.

What most of us miss in using this traditional lens for viewing the financial condition of a business is clarity on the flow of capital in and out of the business. We measure profit and loss for periods of time (income statement) and the status of the capital accounts at a point in time (balance sheet), but most business owners and managers have limited visibility on the critical nature of the actual flow of capital. They know when they do not have sufficient capital to make payroll or pay critical vendors, but that is more the knowledge of critical incidents and not a continuing comprehension of the flow of capital.

One part of the problem in comprehending financial statements lays in the fact that one of the most important financial statements, the financial statement that focuses on cash flow in a business (the Statement of Cash Flows), is not used as extensively as it should be. The Statement of Cash Flows is usually buried deep in "other reports" on most of the accounting systems used by businesses today. I accept personal responsibility for part of this problem. In 1976, when I first wrote the specifications for what became Peachtree Accounting Software, I put the emphasis on the Income Statement and the Balance Sheet, and not the Statement of Cash Flows. Successive generations of Peachtree developers have followed my mistake, as did Peachtree's primary competitor, QuickBooks. It was a natural mistake; in two quarters of financial accounting at Georgia Tech, in the late 1960s, the instructor barely mentioned the Statement of Cash Flow, the focus was on the Income Statement and Balance Sheet. Many courses on accounting and finance today still do not place primary focus on the all-critical flow of funds in a business – they focus on income and expenses and static financial position.

I have observed that a number of online reporters of financial information, Yahoo! Finance for example, do elevate the Statement of Cash Flows to the same level of visibility as the Income Statement and Balance Sheet in providing financial statements for individual companies. But, this equality of presentation still appears to be the exception.

Another part of the problem in comprehending financial statements lays in the fact that we classify cash as an asset, albeit first among assets, like other assets that are actually "uses of cash". Cash is really different from other assets, some of which may produce cash in the future. Cash is the fuel that powers a business. We say, correctly, that "cash is king," but we lump it with accounts receivable, inventory, and other uses of cash on the balance sheet. This point is discussed in more detail in following sections.

I came to appreciate cash and the Statement of Cash Flows only gradually, both as an entrepreneur building businesses and in providing professional services to other business clients. Part of the lack of respect for the Statement of Cash Flows may be that it is conceptually confusing. Most business people are somewhat comfortable with what is shown on the Income Statement (income and expenses and profit and losses over a period of time) and the Balance Sheet (balances at a point in time of the accounts that track assets, liabilities, and equity).

But, the Statement of Cash Flows seems to be harder to grasp. It was originally presented to me as the change in Balance Sheet accounts over time. While this is a true statement, what I gradually came to appreciate is that the Statement of Cash Flows is really a way of visualizing the flow of funds in and out of the business. Put in systems engineering terms, it is a "Statement of Inputs and Outputs of Cash from the Business System." Or, perhaps more useful, it is a "Statement of Sources and Uses of Capital."

The result of this increased appreciation of the Statement of Cash Flows led me to develop the following Capital Flow Model as a systems view of a business:

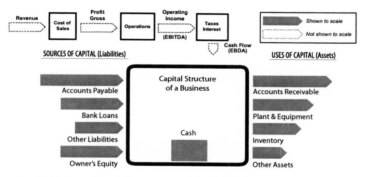

In the Capital Flow Model, <u>Sources of Capital</u> are "inputs" from the left side, <u>Uses of Capital</u> are "outputs" on the right side, cash from operations is either an input (if a profit) or an output (if a loss), as shown at the top. Finally, capital returned to owners in the form of dividends is shown at the bottom as an arrow flowing to the left – back to the equity holders. (Since dividends are rarely returned to owners of small and middle-sized businesses that part of the Capital Flow Model is omitted in most diagrams in this book.) The Flow of Funds diagram is a graphical way of looking at an income statement and a balance sheet, from a systems engineering viewpoint. It is based on what I call "Symbolic Accounting," an improved method for comprehending financial information (patent pending).

As the Capital Flow Model clearly illustrates, what we traditionally call assets are actually "uses of capital" and what we call liabilities and equity are actually "sources of capital." Viewing the flow of funds from an Input and Output viewpoint causes one to question the common view that "assets are good" and "liabilities are bad," which is actually not the case when considering capital in a business. What the Capital Flow Model helps to highlight is that assets are the primary components of what consumes cash and liabilities and equity are important contributors of cash. The operations of a business, of course, are either inputs, if there are operating profits, or outputs, if there are operating losses.

We generally use the term liabilities in a negative sense outside of its use on the balance sheet. If we say "he is a liability for the company," we view that statement as a negative comment about the person. From a balance sheet view, that is the same comment as "he is a source of capital for the company," which produces a very different view. In making this observation, I am not trying to change the definitions of assets and liabilities, but I am trying to help us focus on the true role that liabilities and assets play in the flow of funds in a business. Increasing the capital in a business (increasing cash) is accomplished by only three means: increasing profits, increasing liabilities or equity, or reducing assets, which is clearly illustrated in a graphical manner by the Capital Flow Model.

One result of viewing the capital flows of a business through the lens of the Capital Flow Model is that it can help us focus on the answers to the important questions:

How do I increase the input side most economically?

and

How do I limit the output side without decreasing profits?

We have found the Capital Flow Model to be a very useful tool both in helping experienced managers think about their business and in teaching newcomers to accounting and finance how to visualize what is happening in a business. The experienced managers may even be familiar with the frequently neglected Statement of Cash Flows, but may not have focused on it as a primary view of how the business is operating. The newcomers to accounting and finance usually find the graphical presentation of the income statement and balance sheet presented in the Capital Flow Model easier to grasp initially that the traditional financial statement report view.

One of the benefits of the Capital Flow Model is that it helps to illustrate the differences between sources and uses of capital for different businesses and for businesses in different industries. For example, the average Capital Flow Model for 22 publically listed furniture and fixture manufacturers (two-digit SIC code of 25) is:

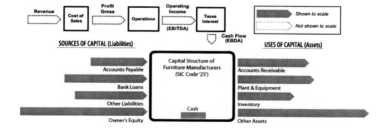

Compare the flow of funds for these 22 furniture manufacturers above with that of 24 publically listed furniture retailers (two-digit SIC code of 57):

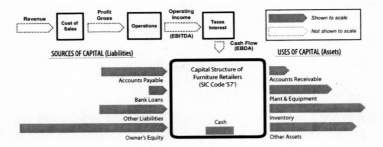

Three important facts are evident from a quick comparison of these two Capital Flow Models:

- The average publically listed furniture manufacturer has more capital invested in funding customers (accounts receivable) than in inventory and almost as much as invested in plant and equipment, and the average retailer has relatively little A/R. The retailer is allowing their customers to buy on credit terms, but that credit has been outsourced to financial institutions.

- Both the wholesaler and the retailer are dependent on their vendors as a source of capital (accounts payable), with the manufactures' A/P about two-thirds of the amount of bank debt and the retailers' A/P more than three times bank debt. This is not surprising, since accounts payable is a free and flexible source of capital. (The thesis of this book is to take advantage of that fact and use it to grow your business and create an enduring loyalty on the part of your business buyer.)

- The accounts payable of the retailers are funded by the accounts receivable of the manufactures, resulting in the large investment by the manufactures in A/R.

The ability of the Capital Flow Model to quickly put into perspective the capital flows of a business is illustrated by comparing the model for Wal-Mart with that for IBM. Wal-Mart's Capital Flow Model is:

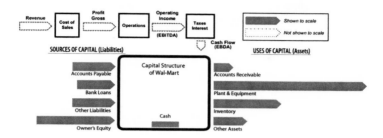

Notice that Wal-Mart has relatively little accounts receivable since it relies on the bank credit card system for providing credit to its customers, while its dependence on accounts payable as a source of capital is second only to the retained earnings component of equity.

On the other hand, the Capital Flow Model for IBM shows that IBM has more invested in supporting sales to customers in the form of accounts receivable than it has invested in inventory and almost as much as it has invested in plant and equipment. IBM's accounts receivable is 25% of its annual sales (90 days of sales outstanding).

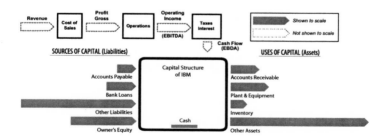

The Capital Flow Model is an interesting and useful tool. FTRANS has posted an interactive version on the web that allows a user to view Capital Flow Models for over 70 industries, organized by two-digit SIC codes. It also allows you to enter your data and then manipulate it to see how changes in inputs and outputs dynamically impact cash. The model is found at www.ftrans.net/cfm.

QUICK HISTORY OF TRADE CREDIT

Quick summary on the history and role of trade credit in enabling commerce; background for using trade credit to grow your business.

Trade credit has been part of commerce for thousands of years. Clay tables from the Babylonian empire provide a list of trade accounts between trading partners. The Code of Hammurabi written in 2250 B.C. sets forth detailed rules for credit transactions between merchants and agents. Trade credit transactions existed before coins and paper money, probably coming shortly after contemporaneous barter transactions. I can picture one early human saying to another, "I will sell you this stone axe today, but you owe me a deer skin by the second full moon".

As commercial trade itself expanded, the use of trade credit expanded. Although some commercial exchanges could be made with an immediate goods for goods transaction, many exchanges had to be made with a temporary, intermediate form of payment and apparently involved the use of agents between the ultimate trading partners. The evidence of a trade credit transaction at one point required a sealed memorandum (probably a clay table with the mark of the agent who owed payment). These intermediate forms of payment evolved into coins, notes, bills of exchange, and our modern banking system.

The use of credit in the exchange of goods was so important that it caused other innovations to be developed to support the growing use of trade credit. One innovation was the double entry system of accounting that enabled accounts to be kept more easily and accurately. The second was the development of banks to issue bills of exchange, provide credit, and generally support commerce, as discussed in the next chapter.

The increase in the sophistication of trade credit is mirrored in the development of accounting. There is evidence that double entry accounts were in use in Genoa as early 1340 A.D. Luca Pacioli, a monk in northern Italy, published a book in 1494 that summarized all of "what is known" about mathematics at the time, including arithmetic, geometry, and proportionality. He included a chapter on the method used by merchants in Venice to keep accounts by the double-entry accounting system that debited and credited offsetting transactions to keep them in balance, the primary method still in use today.

Trade expanded from primarily a local endeavor with the development of trading partners throughout Europe and the Far East during the middle ages. The voyages of Columbus and other early navigators were primarily to open trade routes, rather than exploration for the sake of discovery alone.

Exactly how the split between barter, cash, and credit transactions evolved is an interesting question, one that has not been rigorously studied. What is obvious, however, is that today a vast majority of the value of trade transactions (B2B) are made on credit, with only a small value of transactions made with cash, debt card, or barter.

It is easy to understand why commerce has evolved to this point. First, buyers have learned that sellers will give them credit at no cost. Trade credit rarely involves the payment of interest; in the rare cases where is it specified on invoices for overdue payments, it is even more rarely collected. Second, the timing of the payment is in the hands of the buyer, which enables the buyer to (1) enforce performance on the part of the seller, and (2) have more control on the management of cash. Third, B2B sellers are willing to give trade credit to make sales.

The strategy advocated by this book builds on the fact that trade credit has been part of the fabric of commerce since the dawn of trade. Business buyers expect to receive credit and sellers expect to grant credit. Taking advantage of this fact, especially in a time of limited credit from other sources, can help the properly positioned seller grow sales and profits.

QUICK HISTORY OF BUSINESS BANKING

Quick summary on how banks have supported commerce and how they have shifted in recent years to real estate lending at the expense of supporting trade credit. Explains the Three Cs of lending and how to use that knowledge to improve your access to bank credit.

Banks are mysterious places for most business people. We know that banks are safe places to keep our money. We know that banks are now offering a wide variety of products, many of which are new to banking. We know that banks make loans, although for many of us it is not clear how or why banks make decisions in approving loans.

This chapter will shine a little light on how banks work and, in the process, help provide a better understanding of when banks can be useful for obtaining capital for business growth. This chapter will also explain what is now happing as banks react to the current credit crisis and how that reaction provides both challenges and opportunities.

Another innovation that arose in Italy about the same time as the double entry accounting system (Chapter 4) was a banking system that created the origins of our modern banking system. The Medici family organized a series of banks in Florence and Rome and in other parts of Europe to facilitate trade. The Medici banks had two primary roles. The first role was to allow payments to be made safely for goods that were transported and sold at great distances. The second role was to pay investors (including the church) interest on their deposits and to collect interest from borrowers in the face of edicts from the church that charging interest was a mortal sin. Both of these roles were accomplished by the use of a bill of exchange that allowed a merchant to accept a bill of exchange in pounds issued by the Medici bank in London and convert it to florins when the merchant returned to Florence six weeks later. The bill of exchange system allowed payments to made more securely (you did not have to carry cash long distances through hostile territories), allowed credit to be extended to the buyer by the seller or the seller's bank, and allowed for interest to be charged and earned without everyone being condemned to an eternity in hell.

The Medici banking empire created not only the foundations for our modern checks and paper money (which we still call "bills" today), but also established the idea that banks existed to facilitate commerce. This critical role of banks has continued, primarily with banks being a primary innovator and conduit for payment systems of all types. In addition, banks were a primary source of capital for financing trade transactions, a role that banks played in the United States until fairly recently.

The banking system in the United States developed along two distinct paths, one path relating to the roles of the financial institution and the other path relating to geographic scope of the institution. Each of these two paths saw shifts of tectonic proportions in the past 30 years, shifts that I believe have worked to detriment of small and middle-size businesses.

One of these tectonic shifts occurred in the roles of the institutions. There was once a division in the United States between commercial banks on one hand and thrifts (also called savings and loan or building and loan associations) on the other. Although these two types of financial institutions exist today in a formal sense, the distinction between them is largely in which government agencies regulate the institution and what bodies of law govern, not how they operate. The public today perceives no difference between a commercial bank and a thrift institution, especially since thrifts can now call themselves banks.

Until the roles of banks and thrifts were merged in the late 1970s and early 1980s (which precipitated the savings and loan crisis and federal bail-out of the 1980s), there was historically a significant distinction between banks and thrifts. The classic holiday movie *It's a Wonderful*

Life provides an excellent contrast been a thrift (the Bailey Building and Loan Association) and a commercial bank (Potter's Bank of Bedford Falls). Who can forget the impassioned speech of Jimmy Stewart, playing the role of George Bailey, explaining the role of the Building and Loan to angry depositors seeking immediate withdrawals? Stewart sums it up correctly in the movie; a more complete list of the traditional differences between thrifts and commercial banks is provided in the table below.

Traditional Characteristics of Commercial Banks and Thrifts in the United States (Prior to 1980)		
Characteristic	**Commercial Bank**	**Thrifts**
Typical names	Allowed to use the word "bank" in name.	Savings & Loan, Building & Loan Association, etc. Not allowed to be called a "bank."
Regulated by	Federal: Office of the Comptroller of the Currency State: state bank regulators	Federal: Office of Thrift Supervision (assumed functions of Federal Home Loan Bank Board in 1989) State: state regulators
Insured by	Federal Deposit Insurance Corporation (FDIC) created in 1933 after numerous bank failures	Federal Savings and Loan Insurance Corporation (become insolvent and merged into FDIC in 1989)

Traditional Characteristics of Commercial Banks and Thrifts in the United States (Prior to 1980)		
Characteristic	**Commercial Bank**	**Thrifts**
Deposits	Demand: could be withdrawn on demand in cash or by check	Passbook: required notice (30 or 60 days) to withdraw
Interest on deposits	Not allowed	Allowed
Focus of lending	Primarily business lending, little consumer lending until 1950s, some commercial real estate	Home mortgages
Ownership	Primarily stock; some mutual (depositor owned)	Primarily mutual; some stock
Geographic coverage (branches)	Governed by state law. A few states allowed state-wide branches, most states restricted branches to single city or county only, a few states did not allow any branches.	Governed by state law as well, similar to banks but more restrictive in some states

In the 1980s, under pressure from both the thrifts and the commercial banks to expand their products (the "grass is greener" theory), Congress, state legislatures, and regulators bowed to the industry and virtually erased the distinctions between banks and thrifts. Banks were given more ability to pay interest on deposits and given greater flexibility to make home mortgage loans, thrifts were allowed to offer demand deposit accounts (checking accounts), make business loans, and call themselves banks. The result was a disaster and required massive overhaul of the financial system, insolvency of the thrift insurance system, and billions of tax-payer dollars to rescue the institutions.

At the same time the blending of the roles of banks and thrifts was occurring, the other tectonic shift was also occurring – geographic scope and size of banks was being expanded. Until recently, the ability of a bank to establish branches was governed by state law, even if the bank had a federal charter, and banks could not cross states lines. The states had three general schemes in place. First, a few states, such as North Carolina, permitted state-wide bank branching. (This is the reason that two of the four largest banks in the country, Bank of America and Wachovia, are headquartered in North Carolina – their predecessors were larger and stronger when the avalanche of bank consolidation occurred in the 1990s.) Under the second scheme, most states restricted bank branching to the city or county in which the bank headquarters was located. And, the third scheme, a few states did not permit branches at all.

By the late 1970s, the technology had evolved to permit staff in branches to have remote access to customer financial records. The states began expanding the geographic scope of branches and permitting state-wide branching. At the same time, the states began entering into compacts with other states that basically said, "Your banks can open branches in my state if my banks can open branches in your state". (The law firm I worked for in Atlanta in the late 1970s worked hard on behalf of its major commercial bank client for this set of changes – expanding the roles of banks and intrastate and interstate branching.)

The land rush was on. Larger community banks became regional banks by buying other community banks. The larger regional banks became multi-regional banks. Today, more than 75% of bank deposits are held by the largest 100 banks, less than 1.2% of the 8,561 FDIC insured institutions at the end of September 2007.

There were many changes in banking in the United States as a result of these two shifts. Banking became easier in many ways – I could make a deposit in a Bank of America or Washington Mutual branch in Atlanta for my daughter's college account in New York City. But, these two shifts changed the nature of banking for business, especially small and middle-size businesses (SMB) in ways that were not so positive.

The most important change for the SMB market is that commercial banks shifted from being primarily commercial and industrial lenders to being real estate lenders. Commercial and industrial (C&I) are the loans banks make to businesses that are not secured with real estate. The chart below shows this change by plotting the percentage of commercial bank loans made for C&I and for real estate since the FDIC began reporting the data.

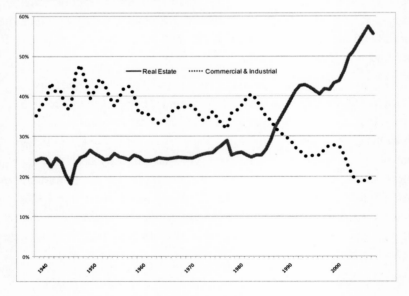

As has been illustrated repeatedly throughout history and is reinforced in the current subprime meltdown, bank lending is not easy. When a bank makes a loan, for each $100 of the loan made (the principal), it hopes to earn about $6.00 of annual interest (at January 2008 rates). Of this $6.00, it is going to pay about $3.00 in interest to the depositors who provided the funds to make the loan (the cost of funds). From the remaining $3.00 or so of net interest margin, the bank has to pay for salaries, facilities, and operating costs which typically take more than $1.75. From the less than $1.25 remaining, the bank has to cover losses on loans that are not repaid in order to make a profit and has to pay taxes on any profits. Therefore, the bank cannot afford to have very many loans not repaid, 1.00% of the original $100 is a problem. (Note: the rapid drops in interest rates during the past 90 days have made these specific estimates a little uncertain, but the basic idea remains the same: banks cannot afford to make many loans that are not repaid.)

When banks make a loan, they are trying to make a decision that allows them to (1) make the loan (they do not earn interest unless they make the loan), and (2) make a loan that will be repaid. While this is an obvious and simplistic statement, it is being made because this paradox for banks is at the core of the current credit crisis and provides the foundation for the strategy promoted by this book of *how to use the credit crisis to grow your B2B business.*

There is an old and common expression in banking that lending decisions should be based on the Three Cs of lending. (There are really about six different Cs that can be inserted into this equation, and different bankers will quote different sets. But, the general meaning is the same.) The Three Cs can help illustrate the difference between C&I and real estate lending and also set the stage for the strategy promoted by this book. A summary of the Three Cs is:

SUMMARY OF THREE CS

Capacity – source of funds to repay the principal and interest on the contracted repayment schedule (also called **cash flow**).

Collateral – secondary source of funds to repay the loan if the capacity is not sufficient.

Character – is the borrower someone we trust (also called **credit**; today this is largely a credit score calculated by a third party).

The Three Cs can be applied (or should be applied) to all types of lending, including commercial and industrial lending and lending on real estate.

Summary of Three Cs – Applied to Residential Real Estate	
Capacity	Does the borrower have a sufficient income (cash flow) to pay the principal and interest on the contracted repayment schedule and still be able to meet other obligations? Can this income be verified from employers?
Collateral	Does the real estate have sufficient value that it can be sold in foreclosure to cover the unpaid principal and interest if the capacity to pay does not continue as planned? Is there an accurate appraisal to confirm the valuation?
Character	Is the borrower someone the bank can trust? (Personal judgment is now replaced with credit scores.)

Obtaining the information to make a decision on a real estate loan is fairly simple – or should be. The mortgage industry developed guidelines for judging how much of a mortgage a person could afford at a given income level. Securing a loan with appraised real estate was traditionally regarded as being safe, provided that the appraisal is done competently and honestly, the market value for real estate does not decline, and there is no fraud in the closing. And consumer credit scores have largely replaced any banker judgment on character or credit.

The information requirements for making a residential real estate loan and the ease with which it can be decisioned are very straight-forward compared to C&I lending:

Summary of Three Cs – Applied to Commercial & Industrial (C&I) Lending	
Capacity	Is the business currently producing sufficient funds (cash flow) to repay the principal and interest on the contracted repayment schedule? Will the business continue to have sufficient income, given its customer base, possible seasonal nature of sales, competition, and a myriad of other parameters that can impact a business, its profitability, and its cash flow?
Collateral	What is the secondary source of funds to repay the loan if the cash flow is not sufficient? What is the value of the assets of the business? Can foreclosed inventory and equipment be sold at a sufficient price to cover the unpaid principal? What is the quality of the accounts receivable; will buyers pay the accounts receivable if the seller is no longer in business or will they try to avoid repayment by claiming disputes?

Summary of Three Cs – Applied to Commercial & Industrial (C&I) Lending	
Character	Is the borrower someone we trust? Can we trust the borrower not to commit fraud and to be competent to keep the business operating?

It is clear in comparing the differences between C&I lending and residential real estate lending that C&I is more complex and requires a banker of considerable experience in gathering and analyzing the information and making an initial decision. C&I lending also requires greater expertise in the on-going monitoring than a residential real estate loan. Because C&I lending is more complex and requires greater expertise, it is a more expensive form of lending, both to initially originate the loan and to monitor the loan throughout its life.

Richard Hartnack, the Vice Chairman of US Bankcorp, in a presentation to a Consumers Bankers Association meeting in October 2007, described the extra cost of originating and monitoring C&I loans as the primary reason why commercial banks have reduced their C&I lending since the 1980s to emphasis real estate lending, which they perceived to be less costly to originate and monitor. (See a graphical representation of what Mr. Hartnack is describing in the chart on page 24 above.)

There is an additional aspect of the cost of C&I lending compared to real estate lending that relates to the consolidation of banks since the 1980s. As the banks consolidated, they centralized the underwriting and decisioning functions for some real estate lending, especially residential real estate. (Commercial real estate is more complex and harder to do well with central underwriting.)

The checklist of information requirements and the analysis required to make the residential real estate loan, theoretically, is very straight-forward and more easily centralized. The information requirements and analyses for C&I is much more complex and frequently depends on parameters that are not easily quantified. (The type of information required for each is summarized in the Three C charts above.) It is hard for an underwriter at a desk in Charlotte to have the same feel for a manufacturing business in Dallas that a C&I lender would have by walking though the factory.

The result of the extra cost of the increased complexity of C&I lending is clear. As the chart on page 24 makes clear, commercial banks have largely left C&I lending as their primary business, especially for the small and middle-sized business market. Most C&I lending today is for businesses larger than $25 million in sales. Most loans to small businesses since 1990 have been secured with either real estate or the personal credit of the owner. This fact means that the funding provided by vendors in the form of trade credit takes on increased importance as banks have become less of a lending source for businesses.

The strategy of growing sales by providing more credit to business buyers on more flexible terms has been valid for thousands of years. However, its value as a growth strategy has been heightened in the past few months by the current credit crisis. This crisis has been caused by the meltdown in the subprime mortgage market, which resulted primarily by lenders not following the Three Cs in making these subprime loans:

Summary of Three Cs – Applied to Current Subprime Mortgage Meltdown	
Capacity	Does the borrower have sufficient income (cash flow) to pay the principal and interest on the contracted repayment schedule? What has now become evident is that many sub-prime borrowers may have been able to make the payments when the "adjustable rate" interest rates were artificially low, but are not able to make the payments when the rates ratchet up per the original schedule.
Collateral	A mortgage on the property allows the bank to foreclose and sell the property to recover the unpaid principal and interest. Great theory when the appraisals were correct in the first place, the market value for housing does not decline, and there is an active market for properties in that price range. However, as we are now seeing, many appraisals were over-stated, market values have declined, and house sales at many price levels are stagnant.
Character	The personal judgment of a banker on the character of a borrower has been replaced with a system of credit scores in recent years. Credit scoring is a new science that works well in general, but still has a number of shortcomings. It will be interesting to see how much of the blame for the mortgage meltdown is laid at the feet of credit scoring in the long run.

The next chapter, Chapter 6, describes how the mortgage melt-down and the credit crisis it spawned will impact most businesses. Chapter 7 describes how to take advantage of this crisis and use the power of trade credit to grow sales and create an enduring loyalty.

THE CREDIT CRISIS AND ITS IMPACT ON BUSINESSES

Quick overview of the current credit crisis and the impact it will have on many businesses, thereby laying the foundation for the growth strategy advocated by this book. How banks will act. How vendors may act. The importance of credit scoring.

The rapid collapse of the subprime mortgage market during the last few months of 2007 has spawned a spreading contraction in the availability of credit in general in the United States and globally. Most banks, including the largest banks and many of the others, have taken hits to earnings and core capital.

This credit crisis will impact most businesses in the United States to some degree especially if the credit crisis does develop into a full-blown recession, as now looks likely. The real culprit in the subprime meltdown appears to be adjustable rate mortgages with artificially-low initial rates ratcheting-up the rate beyond the payment capacity of the borrower. Had this happened more gradually or during a time when the market for new and used homes was increasing, the market might have been able to absorb extra inventory added through foreclosures. In that case, we might have had a foreclosure crisis among the lower income and credit score impaired segments of the population, rather than a general credit crisis.

However, the ratcheting-up of the ARMS interest rates came at a time when the red-hot home building market was already cooling. The market for new and used homes was not sufficiently robust to absorb the extra inventory, which further drove down construction of all types, commercial as well as residential.

Because the construction industry is a large and important part of the economy, the slow-down in home construction impacted many other businesses. The list of other industries impacted by a slow-down in construction is very large and ranges from the building supply chain (manufacturers, distribution, transportation, retailing, etc.) to sub-contractors (HVAC, electrical, plumbing, roofing, etc.) to service providers (real estate sales, appraisers, mortgage processors, title insurers, closing attorneys, etc.) and to others.

The subprime meltdown and the slow-down in construction and related industries are real and will have measurable reductions in those industries. However, the extent of the impact on the rest of the economy to some degree depends on the psychological response of the population. For example, if the home owner thinks "Contractors are not as busy and the price of materials is not going up every month. This is a good time to remodel the family room and install a home theater with 60 inch screen, zillions of speakers, etc." If that home owner then makes that multi-thousand dollar set of expenditures, commerce continues. However, if that home owner is turned-down by their local bank for a home equity line of credit to finance this improvement, optimism is turned into pessimism that may cause the home owner to be more conservative in all purchases, for business as well as personal consumption.

At the time this book went to press (May 2008), the prospect of whether the United States, or other parts of the world, are entering a recession was uncertain, but being widely predicted by many economists. Regardless of whether there is a formal recession (defined as two successive quarters of decline in Gross Domestic Product), it is clear that credit will be less available for most individuals and businesses for 2008 and possibly much longer.

AVAILABILITY AND ACCESS TO CREDIT

The most direct impact of the credit crisis is that lenders are less willing to make loans. This impact has already been seen in real estate lending. Financial institutions of all sizes are taking large write-offs for questionable residential real estate portfolios. But, the credit crisis extends well beyond the subprime mortgage market. Banks and non-bank lenders have significantly tightened their lending standards.

Only the most credit worthy borrowers with conservative projects will be funded for new construction. Only home buyers with good credit will qualify for home mortgages. Banks have been expanding their commercial and industrial lending for the past few quarters (see the upturn shown in the chart on page 24), but it appears that most of the expansion in C&I lending is to larger companies.

The small and middle-size company is facing an even bleaker lending picture than in recent years, and the past dozen years have not been particularly easy. The dilemma can be summarized as follows:

Beginning in the 1970s, for the small and middle-size business (SMB) market, banks began shifting from traditional commercial lending to lending that is based primarily on either (1) the personal credit of the owner and not the business, or (2) real estate. Traditional commercial lending secured with assets of the business has been reduced in importance as a source of business credit due to its high cost and risk to banks, both in originating the loan and in on-going monitoring (See Chapter 5). Business credit cards, with approval based on the personal credit score of the owner, home equity lines of credit on the owner's property, and small unsecured loans with approval based on the personal credit score of the owner have become the major vehicles for bank lending to the SMB market.

The current mortgage-ignited credit crisis has caused banks to become tighter in their standards for first mortgages, home equity lines of credit, unsecured lending, and credit cards. The result is that the sources of bank lending that replaced traditional small business commercial lending are now more difficult to obtain.

As discussed throughout this book, the largest source of capital for more businesses is the funding provided by their vendors (their Accounts Payable). As vendors, both large and small, experience more pressure on their ability to obtain credit for the reasons discussed above, they may be forced to restrict the credit they can grant to their business customers (if they have not read this book and realize that is the wrong thing to do!).

The credit crisis or a recession will reduce overall business activity, resulting in a more difficult environment for the B2B seller. (At the time this book went to press, May 2008, the question of whether the economy was headed into recession depended on which economist you believed. Even if there is not a formal recession, it does appear that 2008 will be a significantly restrained economy compared to 2007.)

The result is a general reduction of the credit available to businesses, both from banks and from vendors. As with other credit contractions, this contraction of credit is likely to impact the small and middle-size businesses more heavily than larger companies.

This reduction in the availability of credit is what creates the strategy opportunity advocated by this book: increase your sales and increase your importance to your business buyers by offering more them credit on more flexible terms.

COST OF CREDIT

One aspect of this credit crisis is that the overall cost of credit is coming down, if you can get approved for credit. The Federal Reserve Board reduced the discount rate three times in the last half of 2007 in an effort to boost the economy, and dropped it 75 basis-points the month before this book went to press. The Fed appears positioned to reduce it further. Commercial banks followed the lead and reduced their Prime Rate (an interest rate from which banks price loans to customers, such as Prime Plus 1.0% or Prime minus 0.5%). These recent rate changes are illustrated by the following chart of key rates:

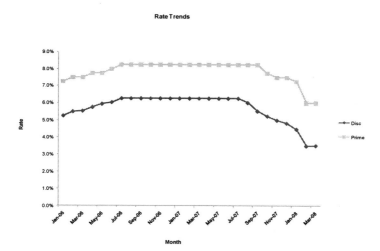

THE IMPORTANCE OF CREDIT SCORING

Credit scoring has completely revolutionized consumer banking in the United States during the past 25 years and is in the process of having a similar impact on business banking as well.

The concept is simple. Collect certain data about individuals relating to how they pay their loans and bills, whether they have filed bankruptcy, and other financial information, and you can develop a score that is a reasonably good predictor of whether they will honor an obligation in the future.

The credit scoring process for consumers has proven to be so reliable that it is almost universally applied for any consumer credit, including real estate, personal loans, and credit cards. The consumer credit score is now also being used, whether really legitimate or not, for making decisions about employment and insurance.

The same concept is also now being used by banks and other financial institutions to credit score businesses. In some cases, the business credit score is linked to the personal credit score of the owner for a "blended score."

The major business credit scoring agencies are:

Dunn & Bradstreet – the traditional trade credit rating agency. Virtually every business in the United States has been assigned a DUNS number and most have credit ratings that are a combination of business size data and trade credit payment histories from reporting vendors.

Equifax – the grand-daddy of consumer credit reporting agencies, originally Retail Credit, Equifax is operating the Small Business Financial Exchange® (SBFE) in cooperation with hundreds of financial institutions. The financial institutions report loan payment data to Equifax, which is combined with some trade credit payment history and other data to calculate a score on the business. In addition, Equifax combines the personal credit scores of the owners with the business score to deliver a blended SBFE score.

Experian – another of the major consumer credit agencies is now publishing a Commercial Inteliscore® for almost all business in the United States.

Business credit scoring is apparently producing good predictors of the potential of default. One bank showed me the summary data they assembled on their existing business customer base when they were evaluating using one of the business credit scoring services. They looked 12 months back at how the business and owner would have be rated in one of the blended scores and plotted that score against whether the business loan actually become more than three months past due during the following 12 months. The resulting data produced a graph that looks like the following (higher scores are shown to the left and lower to the right):

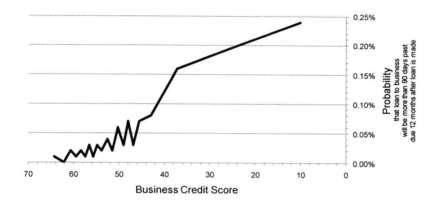

It does not take a financial engineer to see that the potential for default rises dramatically below the blended score of about 44, which makes it easy for this financial institution to establish an absolute cut-off point below which they will not automatically approve the business loan. If the borrower fails to be approved in the credit scoring process, the individual banker can take the loan through the traditional underwriting process. This particular bank has established different requirements for collateral depending on the blended score. The higher scores will permit an unsecured loan to be approved automatically by the system up to a certain dollar level, lower credit scores require additional collateral for security.

Almost all of the top 100 banks in the United States are now using some form of business credit scoring, at least for smaller loans and in many cases to decide if they will even open a deposit account for the business. The trend will continue and I expect that most community banks will also adopt business credit scoring over the next five to ten years. The reality is that credit scoring for businesses is likely to become as pervasive as credit scoring for consumers. The additional reality is that if you and your business do not have high credit scores, your chances of getting a bank loan to fund the strategy advocated by this book are greatly reduced. The good news is that there are viable alternatives to bank loans.

THE POWER OF GRANTING TRADE CREDIT

An overview of how trade credit enables commerce and can grow sales.

Trade credit has been an important part of commerce from the beginning of commercial transactions. Chapter 4 of this book provides a quick outline of the history of trade credit and its role in promoting the creation of the modern banking system (Chapter 5). This Chapter 7 focuses on the power that trade credit provides to enable commerce. This is a power that B2B vendors can use to grow sales and implement the strategy advocated by this book.

The **power of trade credit** manifests itself in two forms:

Reactive power – having sufficient capital to be able to make sales on longer payment terms when <u>required</u> by the buyer (such as Net 60 days). For example, being able to make a large sale to Wal-Mart or Home Depot because they require 60 day payment terms.

Proactive power – being able <u>to offer</u> longer terms to buyers to gain additional sales, which is a key focus of this book.

There is no difference in the practice or funding of reactive trade credit versus proactive trade credit. The difference is only who initiates the discussion of the terms, whether required by the buyer or offered by the seller. Understanding both forms is important, however, in taking advantage of the current credit crisis.

REACTIVE POWER OF TRADE CREDIT

The reactive power of trade credit is having sufficient capital in the business, or access to it, to be able to <u>react</u> to the requirements of a buyer who insists on longer payment terms. Almost all of the larger retailers in the United States and many other large buyers use trade credit as a principal source of their own capital. (See Chapter 3 for a detailed discussion of the importance of trade credit as a source of capital for businesses in the United States.) The reason is simple: trade credit is free and flexible for the buyer. The buyer rarely pays interest on trade credit (certainly not buyers with any leverage on the seller, such as purchasing volume or alternative sources of supply). And, the buyer controls when the payment is made, thereby helping assure performance by the seller and allowing the buyer to manage the outflow of cash.

The following table illustrates how much time several of the major listed companies require to pay for purchases from vendors. The table provides an estimate of DPO (Days Payables Outstanding) calculated from published financial statements. That DPO estimate is simply Accounts Payable at the end of the most recent annual reporting period divided by Cost of Sales for the past year, the traditional calculation for DPO.

Ticker	Name	Revenue $B	DPO
AAP	Advance Auto Parts Inc	4.6	98
AMD	Advanced Micro Devices	5.6	171
APD	Air Products & Chemicals	10.0	77
AMZN	Amazon.com Inc	10.7	80
AAPL	Apple Inc	24.0	114
T	AT&T Inc	63.1	92
BKS	Barnes & Noble Inc	5.3	80
BBI	Blockbuster Inc	5.5	76
BA	The Boeing Co	61.5	118
BGP	Borders Group Inc	4.1	75
BWA	Borg Warner Inc	4.6	82
BMY	Bristol-Myers Squibb Co	17.9	76
CAB	Cabela's Inc	2.1	73
CAJ	Canon Inc	34.9	86
CL	Colgate-Palmolive Co	12.2	69
CMCSA	Comcast Corp	25.0	116

Ticker	Name	Revenue $B	DPO
GLW	Corning Inc	5.2	80
DE	Deere & Co	24.1	120
DELL	Dell Inc	57.4	79
EK	Eastman Kodak Co	13.3	137
LLY	Eli Lilly & Co	15.7	81
EL	Estee Lauder Cosmetics Inc	7.0	65
FRX	Forest Laboratories Inc	3.4	76
DNA	Genentech Inc	9.3	107
GE	General Electric Co	163.4	102
GM	General Motors Corp	207.3	60
HNZ	H.J. Heinz Co	9.0	77
HIT	Hitachi Ltd	87.0	72
INTU	Intuit Inc	2.7	86
JNJ	Johnson & Johnson	53.3	138
JCI	Johnson Controls Inc	34.6	66
KUB	Kubota Ltd	9.6	95
M	Macy's Inc	27.0	111
MOT	Motorola Inc	42.9	61
NWSA	News Corp	28.7	89
NCX	Nova Chemicals	6.7	76
NVS	Novartis	36.0	88
NVO	Novo Nordisk	6.9	65
OXY	Occidental Petroleum	18.2	126
ORLY	O'Reilly Automotive Inc	2.3	91
PSO	Pearson Plc Ads	8.1	65
PFE	Pfizer Inc	48.4	96
PBI	Pitney Bowes Inc	5.7	123
PPG	PGG Industries Inc	11.0	103
QCOM	Qualcomm Inc	8.9	86
Q	Qwest Communications Intl Inc	13.9	65

Ticker	Name	Revenue $B	DPO
RICOY	Ricoh Co Ltd	17.5	104
SNDK	Sandisk Corp	3.3	73
SGP	Schering-Plough Corp	10.6	124
SLB	Schlumberger Ltd	19.2	106
SGR	The Shaw Group Inc	5.7	77
SHW	Sherwin-Williams Co	7.8	65
SI	Siemens	103.4	119
SNE	Sony Corp	70.4	60
S	Sprint Nextel Corp	41.0	76
JAVA	Sun Microsystems Inc	13.9	69
TGT	Target Corp	59.5	61
TEN	Tenneco Inc	4.7	74
TMS	Thomson	7.7	84
TOC	The Thomson Corp	6.6	101
UN	Unilever N.V.	52.3	70
VZ	Verizon Communications	88.1	149
VMED	Virgin Media Inc	7.1	88
WDC	Western Digital Corp	5.5	70
WYE	Wyeth	20.4	73
YUM	YUM! Brands Inc	9.6	71

Having sufficient capital to meet the requirements of providing longer payment terms to buyers that require such terms is the key, of course. That topic is addressed in Chapters 8 through 10.

Even though reactive trade credit is so defined because the seller reacts to the requirements of the buyer, a seller can be proactive in its use. Letting buyers that already require longer payment terms know that you are able to provide those terms, or even longer if it would increase sales, can have a positive impact. First, it may result in securing immediate larger orders. Second, it reinforces the perception by the buyer that you are a strong, financially capable supplier. As buyers for major retailers grapple with suppliers who are facing contractions in available credit and are therefore less reliable, having a vendor step-up and offer more credit and longer terms may be just what the buyer needs to make his or her day.

PROACTIVE POWER OF TRADE CREDIT

The proactive power of trade credit is the principal focus of this book – that is, proactively using trade credit to increase sales and build more enduring relationships with customers.

There are many advantages of the proactive use of trade credit to grow sales, including:

- You control how much you are willing to give.

- It is not very expensive – just the extra cost of interest on the Accounts Receivable for the additional time (if a funding source is available, see Chapter 9 and 10.)

- It is variable cost – you pay for it only as it is being used (except for the small cost to advertise its availability to your customers). Unlike many other ways to grow sales (adding sales staff, advertising, product development, etc.), the cost of granting trade credit is incurred only as it is being used, which is the result of a sale having been made. Making an expense of the business a "variable expense", rather than a "fixed expense" is one of the keys to making your business recession-proof.

There are two disadvantages to using trade credit, both of which can be mitigated by the use of outsourcing accounts receivable, as discussed in Chapter 10:

- You incur additional risk of non-payment by granting more credit on longer terms. This risk has two forms. First, the risk of small customers not paying, which is usually accounted for by taking an allowance (creating a reserve) for expected bad debt.

As long as the non-payments are small (for example, 0.5% to 1.0% of sales), this bad debt can be considered just a cost of doing business. The other risk is more serious – the risk that a large customer does not pay. This risk can wipe out a significant part of earnings for a year and do serious harm to the business. (Both of these components of credit risk can be outsourced to financial institutions, as discussed in Chapter 10.)

- You have to fund the additional time to pay given to the buyer. Doubling the DSO (Days Sales Outstanding – the average time receivables are outstanding) doubles the investment in Accounts Receivable. While the actual interest cost is low for adding the extra days, compared to the extra margin that can be earned, you still have to have the funds available. Methods for calculating this cost is provided in Chapter 9. Securing sources for this extra funding is covered in Chapters 9 and 10.

The proactive power of trade credit can be illustrated by considering four possible offers that could be made by a sofa manufacturer to a furniture retailer:

Offer #1: Buy one sofa wholesale for $400, pre-pay today by cash or check.

Offer #2: Buy one sofa wholesale for $400, pre-pay today by credit card.

Offer #3: Buy one sofa wholesale for $400, pay in 30 days.

Offer #4: Buy two sofas wholesale for $800, pay in 60 days.

From the seller's perspective, each of the alternatives has risks and rewards:

The reward to the seller for **Offer #1** is quick access to the funds, provided that (a) the cash is not counterfeit or an employee does not skim a few bills, or (b) the check is honored by the bank. The manufacturer must pay the costs of accepting and managing payments in cash or by check. These costs and risks can be mitigated by accepting payment only by debit card or by check and immediately converting the check to an ACH transaction. The debit card or ACH conversion will have a cost that depends on the service the manufacturer is obtaining from their merchant services provider and could range from a fraction of 1% to a much higher percentage, depending on how the transaction is being cleared.

The reward to the seller for **Offer #2** is also quick access to the funds for the seller. Accepting a credit card provides for cash in one to three days, but typically carries a cost of somewhere between 2% to 5%, depending on a number of parameters related to the size of the manufacturer and to the transaction itself, including the type of card presented, whether the actual card is presented or just the number given over the phone or Internet, and whether there are any mileage or other rewards offered with the use of the card. If the seller maintains the buyer's card number on file, additional security measures must be observed by the seller, which can add extra cost to comply and for failure to comply. (TJX agreed to pay Visa more than $40 million in late 2007 for failing to maintain proper security on the Visa card numbers of customers.)

The reward to the seller for **Offer #3** is that it may be easier to make the sale and the manufacturer will have access to the funds when the invoice is paid, assuming the check is honored. The risk, of course, is that the retailer does not pay the invoice when it is due and perhaps never pays. The cost to the manufacturer is significant to operate a credit system to assess the buyer's credit before consummating the sale, track the open account to make sure it is paid on time, perform collections if necessary, match the payment to the open invoice and reconcile any differences, pay the cost of capital to have sufficient funds while the Accounts Receivable remains unpaid, and bear the risk of non-payment.

The reward for **Offer #4** is that the manufacturer has earned approximately twice the margin for about the same sales cost as Offers #1 to #3. The labor cost of operating a credit system for an $800 sale is about the same as for a $400 sale, but the carrying cost of capital is higher for the longer time and the perceived risk of non-payment is thought to be higher. (However, our analysis of the payments on tens of thousands of Net 30 Day and Net 60 Day invoices does not indicate a significant difference in default rates). In addition, the primary issue for the seller is that Offer #4 requires an average of twice times as much capital as Offer #3. If the seller has access to ample capital, Offer #4 could generate significant additional sales and margin.

From the buyer's perspective, each of the alternatives also has costs and rewards:

Payment for **Offer #1** is simple; the buyer is finished with the transaction and does not have to track when a payment is due. However, the buyer must fund the transaction with immediately available cash.

Payment for **Offer #2** on a credit card may be the preferred choice for the buyer, especially if the buyer's employer requires purchases on a P-Card or if the buyer wants the rewards offered by the card. The cost to the buyer in paying with a credit card is (a) a strict payment schedule must be observed if interest and penalties are to be avoided and (b) a line of credit with a financial institution is being used, which reduces its availability for other purchases.

Payment for **Offer #3** has advantages for the buyer in receiving an interest free loan for 30 days and the buyer controls when payment is made. This control of the payment is important for the buyer for two reasons. First, it gives the buyer leverage to extract performance from the seller (time to receive the sofa and make sure it is the right style and color and have not been damaged in shipment). Second, it lets the buyer control its cash outflow more carefully. Sellers routinely accept payments a few days late, or even many days late, and continue to sell to those buyers, providing the buyer considerable flexibility on when payment is actually make.

Payment for **Offer #4** is particularly attractive for the buyer, since the buyer, in addition to the controlling the time of payment discussed in #3 above, has time to place the sofas on the showroom floor and perhaps be sold before the payment is due. The "interest free loan" of $800 that the manufacturer makes for 60 days means that the retailer does not have to obtain that capital from another source.

This simple description of four possible offers by a seller illustrates the range of risks and rewards for both sellers and buyer in using trade credit. It also illustrates the power that proactively offering more trade credit can have in encouraging more sales.

I first became aware of the significant proactive power of trade credit when I organized a consolidation of sales agencies in the home furnishing industry in the late 1990s. These sales agencies are the outsourced sales force for manufacturers and importers, both large and small. The sales agencies receive a commission of between 10% and

15% of the wholesale price of the goods they sell to retailers on behalf of manufacturers. The consolidation was accomplished in part by using trade credit to acquire target companies, as discussed in detail in Chapter 11. We acquired 23 sales agencies employing a total of about 350 sales reps, representing about 600 manufacturers, and selling about $600 million annually for these manufacturers. The financial strategy was based in part on growing commission revenue of the acquired agencies.

We tried a variety of mechanisms to help our manufacturers grow sales, which would also grow our commissions. We conducted extra product training to make the sale reps more knowledgeable about their lines. We used database analysis to target retailers. We provided extra incentives for sales reps and provided rebates for retailers. What we discovered was that a simple tool proved to be the most effective: offering longer payment terms for larger orders. Just as in the sofa example above, offering 60 day payment terms, or longer, would produce more sales.

We would frequently structure the offerings in steps: "For orders up to $1,000, net 30 day terms. For orders between $1,000 and $3,000, net 60 day terms. For orders over $3,000, net 90 day terms." The results were immediate and almost always certain. When we posted terms like these at the wholesale markets in New York, Chicago, Atlanta, Dallas, San Francisco, and other cities, the results were the same: sales would go up. We could expect at least a 15% to 20% lift in show orders for the manufacturers offering these terms, and frequently higher.

The problem we encountered was that the program worked too well and many of our manufacturers could not fund the increased credit required. (The recognition of this dilemma eventually resulted, several years later, in the creation of FTRANS and Trade Credit Express as a solution, as discussed in Chapter 10.)

The power of this offering was reinforced to me a few years after we sold the consolidated firm when I ran into one of my former sales managers at the High Point furniture market. At the time, he was the VP of sales for a middle-sized furniture manufacturer in North Carolina. He reported that he had taken the "longer payment terms mean increased sales" strategy to the next level: his firm had replaced their traditional Net 30 days for an opening order of $1,000 with Net 180 days for an opening order of $5,000, and the results were spectacular. The furniture retailer achieved two primary outcomes with the longer payment terms:

- The retailer could purchase enough of the manufacturer's line of products to show an entire room arrangement, not just a representative piece of two.

- The retailer had ample time to sell product and reorder more inventory before they were obligated to pay for the initial opening order.

The manufacturer concluded the additional margin on the larger sale more than covered the extra cost of the credit risk and funding the sale for an additional four or five months. In addition, being able to offer longer payment terms demonstrated financial strength on the part of the seller. (This manufacturer was owned a private equity firm that was willing to invest in growth and did not have the problem of funding trade credit faced by most manufacturers in the industry.)

The success enjoyed by this furniture manufacturer in offering proactive trade credit can be replicated by many businesses, without being owned by a private equity firm (the most expensive source of capital – see Chapter 9). But, it also highlights the key issue in using the strategy: using extended payment terms to grow sales increases both the risk in granting the credit and the amount of capital required.

The next three chapters of this book address these issues. Chapter 8 discusses the cost of implementing this strategy. Chapter 9 discusses the traditional methods for increasing the source of capital to execute the strategy. Chapter 10 discusses the newly available method of trade credit outsourcing, which allows the seller to reduce both the risk and funds required to offer trade credit to business buyers.

CAN I AFFORD TO GIVE MORE TRADE CREDIT?

How to calculate the benefit to cost ratio of offering longer terms and how much additional capital is required, if any.

If you answer affirmatively the question "Can I sell more by offering longer payment terms?" your second question should be "How much will it cost and can I afford to offer longer terms?"

The answer to the cost question is that offering longer payment terms is surprisingly inexpensive – if you have access to the capital to fund the sales. For example, a small wholesale distributor with $1,000,000 of annual trade credit sales on a Net 30 Days basis might boosts sales by 10% ($100,000) by offing Net 60 days terms on larger orders. The incremental cost is very affordable. For example, this business owner might calculate her direct incremental cost as:

Additional revenue	$100,000
Cost of goods sold	($60,000)
Gross profit	**$40,0000**
Interest on $100,000 of sales for an extra 30 days at 18% annual interest	($1,500)
Printing, postage, and phone calls to tell customers of increased terms	($1,000)
Increased administrative time to track and collect A/R (0.5%)	($500)
Increased bad debt risk (0.5%)	($500)
Increased risk of significant non-payment (1.5%)	($1,500)
Total additional costs	**($5,000)**
Total incremental profit	**$35,000**

This simple example may not present margins and costs that are representative of your business, but it is offered to illustrate four points:

- First, the incremental margin opportunity for increased sales by offering longer payment terms may be quite high.

- Second, there are costs associated with increasing sales and in operating a credit system.

- Third, there is a risk premium in any credit transaction that is more than just historical bad debt cost (this is the risk of the major customer default that has not yet happened).

- Fourth, there is a cost of capital and it is usually higher that most people think.

The simple example above indicates that our wholesale distributor could increase her earnings by about $35,000 on $100,000 in incremental sales, a very attractive proposition, provided that she can access the extra working capital of $100,000 for an additional 30 days and she does not suffer a major credit default. In the real world, not all the $100,000 sales would come instantly, but would be spread over some time period. However, as discussed in Chapter 7, our experience with offering extended payment terms in certain industries is that it does produce a very quick response. Chapters 9 and 10 provide alternatives for dealing with funding the increase in working capital and Chapter 10 provides an alternative for outsourcing the risk of a credit default.

CREDIT RISK

I stress the risk aspect of the strategy proposed by this book because it is a significant, but under-appreciated, threat to any business that operates an internal credit system. (Chapter 10 describes how to outsource this risk.) Most small and medium-size businesses do not employ credit analysts and collection professionals. Yet, the credit function is frequently the largest investment made by a trade credit seller. (As discussed in Chapter 3 above, more than 60% of trade credit sellers in the United States have Accounts Receivable as their largest use of capital.)

The simple example above has two lines in the cost model for credit risk. The first is the traditional bad debt cost that most trade credit sellers experience to some degree on a regular basis. For most trade credit sellers, this cost is usually quite small.

The second cost line related to credit risk is the risk that one or more major customers will default on their credit to vendors. Thankfully, this is a cost that most businesses never actually experience, just as most businesses never experience a loss due to fire. Yet, this credit risk is a real and continuing risk for any business that operates a credit system, especially since most businesses have no mechanism for monitoring the ongoing credit-worthiness of their customers. As the economy declines, this risk will increase.

My own experiences with credit risk over nearly 50 years of granting credit mirrors what most trade credit sellers see. I have personally experienced a modest amount of bad debt write-offs directly, and have seen at close hand several cases where the credit default of customers killed a business. My own personal experience with credit defaults began when I was 11 years old and delivering the Atlanta Journal and Constitution newspapers in Waycross, Georgia. The AJC paper boys purchased the newspapers from the local distributor and resold them to customers on our route. We had to collect from each customer, usually monthly. (This was before the wide-spread adoption of bank credit cards and it was common for most retailers, including paper boys, to give credit.) If a subscriber was not home and I could not collect, I learned that I had to continue to deliver newspapers until I could catch up with them and collect the couple of dollars for the month. Meanwhile, I still had to pay each week for the newspapers being delivered. You would like to think that people would not "stiff" the paper boy, but they did.

The most painful personal experience of a business failure due to credit default of a customer occurred to a close family member. He operated a wholesale distribution business selling packaging materials to fruit and vegetable growers in the southeast. He was a very careful businessman and tried to run the business conservatively. He purchased a credit reporting service that rated growers and he would not extend credit to anyone that did not have a good rating. After 10 years of successful operation, he had built the business to nearly $1 million in annual sales and was beginning to see a reasonable profit. Then, an onion grower went bankrupt and defaulted on the payment of $85,000 for mesh onion bags and really left my family member holding the bag. The bankrupt grower was a third-generation farmer and had a good credit rating according to the credit service. The damage to my family member's business was fatal. Although he did not have to declare bankruptcy, he did have to close the business, with several of his vendors also taking losses. He paid on a personally guaranteed SBA loan for more than 10 years after closing the business.

Chapter 10 describes a new mechanism for outsourcing trade credit business processes, including outsourcing the credit risk. If you outsource the credit function, you have eliminated the risk of your business failing due to the credit default of major customers. If you elect not to outsource the entire credit function, at a minimum you should find and subscribe to one or more business credit rating services – and hope they are better than the one rating fruit and vegetable growers in the southeast.

COST OF CAPITAL

The example above uses 18% as a cost of capital, which might strike you as high in this time of low interest rates, but may actually be a very conservative estimate. Most small and medium-size businesses do not have an accurate estimate of their true cost of capital. For most businesses, the answer probably should be "What would it cost me to get that next X dollars of capital?" If the business in our example has an extra $100,000 sitting in a savings account, the cost of capital may be related to the interest that would have been foregone on the savings account. (Even in this case, the real cost of capital is more than just the lost interest; it also includes the cost of not having those funds immediately available for some other purpose.) However, if the capital has to be obtained from another source, the cost could be quite a bit higher, as discussed in more detail in Chapters 9 and 10.

CONCLUSION

After reviewing the benefits of the increased margin to the costs, most trade credit sellers will probably conclude that they can afford to offer longer terms, provided they have some way to fund the increased working capital required and to manage the increased risk.

HOW TO FUND: INCREASE THE INPUT

Increase your source of capital to fund the increase in A/R by the traditional methods: vendors, banks, receivables financing, and equity.

Earlier sections of this book, in particular Chapter 3, have discussed the Capital Flow Model of a business, which illustrates the source and use of funds in the enterprise. This chapter discusses how to increase the inputs of the model – the sources of capital on the left side.

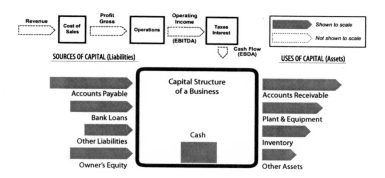

The following sections discuss how to increase the amount of working capital available by increasing the sources of capital, which is the traditional alternative for having the funds to grant more trade credit to buyers.

INCREASED FUNDING FROM VENDORS

As pointed out in this book several times, funding by vendors (Accounts Payable) is the largest source of capital for more businesses in the United States than any other source, more than loans from financial institutions, investment by owners, or any other source. As previously discussed in Chapters 3 and 7, the reasons are simple: trade credit is free and it is flexible –the buyer pays no interest and controls the time of payment. It is also great place to start in looking for additional capital on the input side with which to fund increased trade credit granted to your buyers.

The answer to the question "how do you get more funding by vendors extending longer payment terms?" is easy: ask for it. Most sellers, at least the ones that have not yet read this book, are reactive – they are going to give longer payment terms only to buyers that require it. But, what if you are not the size of Wal-Mart or Home Depot or another retailer that can demand longer payment terms. No matter, still ask for the longer terms. But, do so in a way that shows the vendor how they benefit. For example, the following statement positions the request for longer terms as a win-win for both parties:

> This credit crisis is presenting us with a great opportunity to increase sales by offering longer payment terms to our buyers. We would like to include the products we buy from you in this offer for longer payment terms, and would like for you to participate by increasing the payment terms that you provide us from Net 30 Days to Net 75 Days.

The above statement applies directly to the supply chain for goods, but similar statements can be crafted for a variety of services as well.

What if the vendor says: "Sorry, but I cannot afford to give you longer terms, even if it would results in higher sales."? Send them a copy of this book. And, consider how important this vendor is to you and what the impact on your business would be if they go out of business. The inability of being able to offer extended terms to you could be sign of financial weakness. (Conversely, offering longer terms to your buyers is a sign of your strength.)

The tactic of obtaining longer terms from vendors works in many situations, but not all. The next sections describe other alternatives.

INCREASED FUNDING FROM BANKS

Banks are a logical place to seek increased capital to fund the granting of additional trade credit to buyers, but they may not be a successful source (unless they are participating in trade credit outsourcing, as discussed in Chapter 10). As discussed in Chapter 5, banks have largely moved away from funding small and medium-sized enterprises based on the assets of the business and have replaced it with lending based on the credit of the owner and secured with real estate.

Asking your bank for a new line of credit, or an increase in your current line, to fund additional trade credit sales might be worth the time to make the request. Even if you are turned down in your request, the experience could be useful in gaining additional insight into how the financial markets are viewing the current credit crisis. This will help you understand what your buyers are facing in their need for capital and how offering more credit to them could be of great benefit.

There is one downside to asking for additional bank credit and being turned down (in addition to the feeling of rejection), which is that most bank credit today is based on the personal credit score of the owner and the bank credit inquiry on your personal credit could lower your score. The credit scoring models implemented by the major credit bureaus (Equifax, Experian, and Trans Union) and used by most banks may count a query for new credit as a negative in computing the next credit score. If you are going to ask banks for more credit, do not ask more than one or two – the result may be one of diminishing returns as each request results in successively lower credit scores for a period of time.

If you are going to ask your bank, however, review the Three Cs of lending, discussed in detail in Chapter 5, which provide a framework for how your bank will view your request, even if they do not formally incorporate the Three Cs in their credit policy.

Summary of Three Cs – Applied to Requesting Additional Bank Credit	
Capacity	Does the borrower have sufficient income (cash flow) to pay the principal and interest on the contracted repayment schedule? You should be able to make a case for the additional cash flow to cover the increased line that will result from increased sales, especially if the line is structured as one secured by Accounts Receivable – you will only have an increased need to fund A/R as sales increase.
Collateral	This is usually the problem area – most banks will not count A/R as collateral since they have little visibility on the credit quality of the buyer and your ability to manage a credit system. This may be offset by their willingness to make the loan based on a higher credit score.
Character	The personal banker-judgment of character has largely been replaced in banking with a credit scores in recent years – if you have a good personal credit score, your chances are improved for an increased business credit line.

ASSET BASED LENDING

One form of commercial lending by banks is called asset based lending. Asset based lending (ABL) is a commercial line of credit in which the collateral is assets of the business, usually accounts receivable and perhaps inventory. (The capacity and character aspects of the Three Cs are the same as above.) The bank is able to gain comfort in holding these assets as collateral through close monitoring of the assets. For example, it is not unusual for the bank to require the business to file a borrowing base certificate by which management certifies the precise collateral eligible to obtain advances under the line of credit. The lender will frequently require monthly financial statements, which are carefully scrutinized, and quarterly or annual audits. This type of lending is generally more expensive to originate and administer than an unsecured line of credit or a term loan. The extra cost of originating the loan and administering it, including the quarterly or annual audits, is passed on to the borrower. But, ABL lending is frequently less expensive than receivables discounting or the cost of an equity investment.

Due to the cost of originating and administering the loan, most banks and non-bank ABL lenders have set fairly high thresholds for granting ABL loans. For example, many lenders have a minimum of $2 or $3 million for an ABL line of credit, which implies a business of $20 million or more in annual trade credit sales, a number that represents less than 0.3% of all businesses in the United States.

The cost to the borrower of an ABL line is typically made up of several components, including:

- Interest on advances, which is frequently a variable rate based either on the bank's Prime Rate or the London Inter-Bank Offer Rate (LIBOR), which is usually a couple of percentage points below the Prime Rate. Interest may be quoted as a percentage above or below Prime or above LIBOR, such as Prime Plus 2.0% which means that interest for that period (daily, monthly, etc.) is based on an annual interest rate equal to the current Prime Rate plus 2.0%. If Prime at the moment is 6.0%, the Prime Plus 2.0% would be 8.0% annually, or 0.0222% per day, using 360 days as the calculation base. Adjustments to the base rate may also be quoted in Basis Points – there are 100 basis points to the percent.

For example, LIBOR Plus 225 basis points is the same as LIBOR Plus 2.25%.

- Fees, which can be calculated on a number of different measures, such as an origination fee based on the total loan approved or the amount of the approved line that is not currently being used.

- Out of pocket costs, such as the cost of the auditor, etc.

RECEIVABLES DISCOUNTING OR RECEIVABLES FINANCING

During the past 25 years a specialized form of lending for small and medium-sized businesses has become more popular, due largely to banks decreasing their commercial lending to this market. Called receivables financing, receivables discounting, or recourse factoring, this form of lending is generally provided by non-bank financial institutions, although a few banks do make these types of loans. Receivables discounting is discussed in detail in this section since it is frequently the only alternative available for many small and middle-sized businesses. (See the road map for navigating the alternatives in Chapter 13.)

Receivables discounting could be considered a form of small ticket asset based lending in that it uses the Accounts Receivables as collateral for the loan, and may have many of the attributes of ABL, such as very close monitoring. However, receivables discounting is usually priced in a manner that is different from ABL pricing. Whereas the primary cost for an ABL line is calculated as a rate of interest on the outstanding balance (i.e., Prime Plus 2.0%) plus fees, the cost of the receivables discounting is frequently quoted as a discount from the face amount of the invoice applied for each fraction of a period of time the invoice remains unpaid, such as 2.0% for each 30 days. For an invoice paid on the 61st day, the discount would be 6.0%. This can be a fairly high rate of interest, especially since the lender is typically advancing only a percentage of the invoice amount

(75% or 80% is typical) while changing the discount on the full invoice amount.

The best way to obtain an accurate estimate of the cost of receivables discounting is to sum the invoices paid within each period for which different discount amounts apply. For example, if the charge imposed by the receivables discounter is 2.0% per each 30 days invoices are outstanding, or fraction thereof, the following distribution of invoices would result in the indicated charges:

Period	First 30 days	31 to 60 days	61 to 90 days	Over 90 days*	Total
DSO for Period	25	40	62	91	
Fee % for Period	2.0%	4.0%	6.0%	8.0%	
% Paid in Period	10%	60%	20%	10%	
$ Paid in Period	100,000	600,000	200,000	100,000	1,000,000
Weighted DSO	2.5	24.0	12.4	9.1	48.0
Fee $ for Period	2,000	24,000	12,000	8,000	46,000
Weighted Discount	0.2%	2.4%	1.2%	0.8%	4.6%

* Charged back to seller after 90 days (recourse)

The average A/R outstanding during the year on $1 million in sales on a DSO of 48 days (13.2% of the year) would be $132,000. If the discounter was advancing 80% of the A/R, the average outstanding loan would be $105,200 for which $46,000 in fees would equal 43.7% annual interest.

The equivalent interest rates on receivables discounting charges for several examples are provided in the table below. (These examples assume the advance rate is 80% of the face amount of the invoice. DSO means Days Sales Outstanding and is the average number of days that invoices are unpaid.)

Example	Discount % Per 30 Days	Average DSO	Total Discount %	Equivalent Annual Interest Rate
1	1.0%	48	2.3%	29.9%
2	1.5%	48	3.2%	30.4%
3	2.0%	48	4.6%	43.7%

Determining the actual cost of receivables discounting may not be as simple as the above examples, however, since many of the contracts are quite convoluted. Whether this is a deliberate effort to hide the true cost of this type of lending or just industry conventions that have evolved over many years is difficult to determine. It may be that the pricing as a discount rather than quoting an actual interest rate was developed in an effort to circumvent state usury laws regulating the maximum amount of interest that can be charged. However, since the usury laws of most states have become so lax in recent years, this may not be the continuing motivation. (The usury limit in my home state of Georgia is currently 5% monthly – 60% annually without compounding, and most business loans are outside the scope of the usury laws entirely.)

Another motivation for quoting the pricing as a discount, rather than as interest, may be to further support the proposition that the lender is "buying" the invoice from the seller. However, since receivables discounting almost always requires the seller to repurchase any invoices that are not paid within a defined time period, such as 60 or 90 days after the due date, they are not a true "purchase and sale" of the accounts, but only a form of lending. A true sale would require that risk of non-payment be passed to the buyer of the invoice, that is the sale of the invoice be made on a non-recourse basis and not be charged back to the seller for non-payment. Part of the motivation for describing receivables discounting in terms of buying invoices rather than lending may be an effort to avoid having to qualify as a lender in certain states.

One confusing aspect in evaluating receivables discounting to other alternatives is the nomenclature. Many receivables discounters refer to themselves as "factors" or perhaps "recourse factors". Receivables discounters are essentially lenders that have a security interest in the accounts receivable as their collateral. Just as with any other loan, the advance from the discounter is properly booked by the seller as a loan under liabilities and the seller continues to show the accounts receivable as an asset until paid.

The confusion in nomenclature exists because the traditional definition of "factor" means non-recourse. A traditional factor or true factor, as described in more detail in Chapter 10, actually does purchase the account (represented by an invoice) and assumes the risk of non-payment due to the financial inability of the buyer to pay. The basic act of a merchant accepting a credit card for payment is actually true factoring. In true factoring, an advance by the factor is really early payment of the account and not a loan from the viewpoint of the seller (although it may be booked as a loan on the books of the factor).

The confusion is created because many receivables discounters are now calling themselves factors. In fact, one of the trade associations representing receivables discounters has the word factoring in its name (International Factoring Association). The important issue is not the words factor or factoring, but what service the financial institution is actually providing.

Three things can be said about receivables discounting:

- It is generally an expensive way to borrow capital; the cost of funds is significantly higher than typical unsecured bank lines or asset based lending.

- Receivables discounting may be the only option available for many small businesses, especially as banks have exited commercial lending for the small and middle-sized business market.

- Even with its high relative cost, receivables discounting may still be an economic way to grow sales by offering buyers longer payment terms. Even if you triple the interest cost in the example in Chapter 8, the benefits of increased margin from increasing sales is still significant.

EQUITY FUNDING

The fourth capital input or source of funds in the Capital Flow Model is equity, whether an actual equity investment for the purchase of stock or a loan from friends and family.

Equity may be both the most expensive source of capital and the most difficult to obtain. Equity is expensive because you are giving up a share of the future operating profits of the business and a share of the capital gains should the business ever be sold. In addition, you may be giving up some control of the business due to requirements imposed by the investor. While many lenders, whether banks or receivables discounters, impose some restrictions, they may not be as severe as the restrictions imposed by investors. In addition, lender limitations disappear when the loan is repaid; investors are usually with you until the business is sold or you find a way to buy them out.

Raising outside equity to grow certain companies may be a necessity. The advice to avoid outside equity may seem a little gratuitous since I have raised over $170 million of capital for startup companies that I have started. My current company is funded by high quality institutional investors and would not have established certain key relationships without their help. Despite this reliance on outside equity, I still support the view that outside equity should be your last resort as a source of capital.

Calculating the real cost of raising capital by selling equity is beyond the scope of this book, but a simple example illustrates how expensive equity can be. Assume that your business has $10 million in sales, has a gross margin of 40% ($4 million), has a fixed operating cost of $3 million, and is making an operating profit of 10% ($1 million). You believe you can increase your sales by 50% over the next four years (11% annual compounded growth) without increasing the fixed operating cost or impacting the gross margin, at which point your gross margin on $15 million of sales would be $6 million and operating profit would be $3 million. In other words, a 50% increase in sales can result in a 200% increase in operating profits.

To increase sales 50%, you estimate that you need an additional $1 million of capital. If you raise $1 million of equity, it will probably require giving up 20% to 33% of the company (if company is valued at $3 million to $5 million, a pre-investment operating profit multiple of 3X to 5X). The net present value (the sum of the future earnings discounted at some value) of this 20% to 33% of your future earnings that you have given up could be significantly greater than the cost of obtaining a bank loan for $1 million or even a loan from a receivables discounter. In addition, the effort required to find an investor for most small companies, and go through the analysis, due diligence, and closing, is very time consuming and costly compared to the time and expense required to pursue the other alternatives.

In any event, obtaining capital to fund an increase in Accounts Receivable by raising equity takes entirely too long to be a useful tactic to pursue the strategy promoted by this book.

HOW TO FUND: OUTSOURCE TO INCREASE THE OUTPUT

Outsourcing A/R functions is a way of reducing risk, cost, and capital required. A new method of outsourcing trade credit allows the small and middle-size business to increase the A/R granted to buyers while reducing the capital required to fund A/R.

Chapter 7 describes the opportunity to use the current credit crisis to grow sales by offering business buyers more credit. Chapter 8 discusses financial aspects of offering additional trade credit to customers and how to evaluate the benefits to the costs. Chapter 9 discusses several alternatives for increasing the "input side" of the Capital Flow Model, including the most economical source of capital, funding by vendors (increasing accounts payable).

This Chapter 10 discusses the "output side" of the Capital Flow Model and how to fund more output by reducing output. This seeming contradiction is achieved by outsourcing parts of the trade credit system to financial institutions. The basic concept is simple – it is very similar to accepting a credit card for payment. The business processes related to operating a trade credit system, including evaluating and managing risk, administration, and collections, can be performed on a much larger scale and for lower cost by financial institutions than the cost of performing these functions in an individual business. Also, financial institutions have a much lower cost of capital, especially banks with federally insured deposits.

OUTSOURCING OF CONSUMER CREDIT

Fifty years ago it was very common for retailers to operate their own credit systems in much the same way that business to business sellers of all sizes operate their trade credit functions today. In 1945, half of all consumer credit in the United States was funded by the retailers themselves and half by financial institutions. In 1966, Bank of

America introduced a financial innovation that has permitted virtually all retailers to outsource their credit systems, and today more than 97% of consumer credit is funded by financial institutions. The financial innovation introduced in 1966 was the national expansion of the BankAmericard credit card program by dividing the risk between two different financial institutions, which permitted the card system to go not only nationwide, but global. (In addition to the financial innovation of dividing the risk introduced by Bank of America, three other innovations permitted the creation of the national and then international credit card system. First, the introduction of main frame computers provided sufficient horsepower to process transactions. Second, the introduction of direct dialing (no manual operator intervention) permitted long distance rates to be reduced to a level that it was economic to verify a credit card transaction. Third, the consolidation of retail credit agencies permitted banks to better evaluate buyers to whom they issued cards.)

The financial innovation introduced by Bank of America over 40 years ago not only revolutionized consumer credit, it provides important insights and opportunities for trade credit sellers today.

Prior to the BankAmericard innovation, bank credit cards involved only three parties: the seller, the buyer, and a single financial institution (as American Express and Discover continue to operate today). This single financial institution has credit risk on the buyer, which is the risk that the buyer will not pay for the credit transaction. It also has the risk of sponsoring the seller, also called the merchant. This risk on the merchant is frequently called the "fraud and unresolved dispute risk" and relates to the fact that a financial institution has advanced the payment on the transaction to the merchant. If the merchant goes out of business or is otherwise unable to honor disputes with the buyer, the financial institution may have to absorb the cost of the disputed transaction. In a similar manner, if the merchant submits fraudulent transactions, the financial institution is at risk since it has advanced the funds, but will be unable to collect from the buyer.

The first bank credit card program was created in 1946. For the next 20 years, a number of banks created three party card programs, but the rate of adoption was limited. As discussed in Chapter 5, prior to the 1980s, banks were not permitted to branch beyond limited geographical areas, such as counties or, in a few cases, entire states. Banks felt comfortable approving only merchants and buyers that were in their local service area. As a result, the card programs were only local in scope.

The Bank of America innovation in 1966 was to create a five-party network of financial institutions around the BankAmericard. In addition to the seller (the merchant) and the buyer, the new system divides the responsibilities of the financial institutions into three parts. One bank sponsors the buyer and is called the issuing bank because it issues the card. The issuing bank has the credit risk on the buyer. A second bank sponsors the merchant and has the fraud and unresolved dispute risk on the merchant and is called the merchant acquiring bank. The fifth party is the interchange, or the BankAmericard network. In addition to the these five primary parties, there are a number of selling agencies, processors on the merchant side, processors on the issuing side, and others that may be involved.

What Bank of America created was an immediate success. First National Bank of Atlanta could issue a BankAmericard to one of its customers and that customer could have the card accepted for payment by merchants in hundreds of other cities, each merchant sponsored by a different bank. Within two years, there were card holders and merchants in all 50 states and in many countries in Western Europe. A competing network of banks created the Master Charge system, which in 1977 was renamed MasterCard. Also in 1977, BankAmericard was renamed VISA.

At first, merchants added the bank credit cards as a fourth payment method, in addition to accepting cash, checks, and their own internal credit systems. The retailers accepted the cards for payment in order to build sales. The banks mailed millions of BankAmericard and Master Charge cards to consumers without an application from the consumer. The Federal Trade Commission put a stop to that practice in 1972, but in the meantime these new card holders would walk into a store and ask, "Do you accept this card?". Merchants began accepting cards to capture these new sales opportunities.

Gradually, however, retailers came to realize that accepting payment by a credit card was easier and less expensive than operating an internal credit system. Retailers of all sizes began dropping their internal credit systems in favor of the bank card systems. Even Sears Roebuck & Co., which at one time operated the world's largest consumer credit system, sold their card program to a financial institution.

When you consider the convenience of accepting a credit card for payment compared to operating an internal credit system, it is easy to understand why retailers were willing to make the switch.

TRADE CREDIT VS. CONSUMER CREDIT

However, during this 40 year period when almost all retailers swapped their internal credit systems for a bank card system, very few trade credit sellers have made the switch. In the United States, more than 97% of consumer credit is funded by financial institutions and less than 3% of consumer credit is granted through in-house credit systems operated by retailers. At the same time, less than 3% of trade credit is transacted through the bank card system and more than 97% of trade credit is granted through in-house credit systems operated by B2B sellers. (The symmetry of these numbers is purely coincidental.) That is a striking difference: almost universal acceptance of the bank card system for consumer credit compared with an almost universal rejection of the card system for trade credit.

The banks, VISA, MasterCard, American Express, and Discover would argue that the use of credit cards for trade credit is growing every day. And, they are right, but only by insignificant amounts. Whether due to increased adoption of the purchasing card by businesses for the convenience of making small purchases or the advantages of outsourcing an internal credit system, the amount of trade credit transacted on credit cards is growing, but the relative amount is very small. Of the $19 trillion in trade credit transactions in the United States in 2007, less than $550 billion was on credit cards; $550 billion is a big number, but is less than 3% of trade credit transactions.

VISA ran a two-page advertisement in the Wall Street Journal in late 2007 that bragged that $340 billion of global business transactions are made through the VISA system. The 10 zeros in that number were each in the form of a globe and the $340,000,000,000 stretched across both pages of the WSJ. It is an impressive advertisement. However, global trade credit sales are estimated to be in excess of $60 trillion annually; the amount transacted on VISA is approximately 0.5% of the global total (an amount my wife would call "budget dust").

If the bank card system has been so successful in capturing consumer credit, why has it been unsuccessful in capturing trade credit? The answer to this question is more than academic. The answer to this question is important for many reasons. One important aspect of this answer is that the current trade credit system is inefficient. The current system has about half the total trade credit in the United States granted by small and middle-size businesses whose cost of operating credit systems is higher than the cost if financial institutions operated the system. It is also the reason that using trade credit to grow sales *works* and the reason that this book was written. The fact that trade credit sellers have *not* outsourced their trade credit functions to the bank credit card system now puts them in a position to use trade credit as a tool to grow sales.

The question of why this huge gap exists between the outsourcing of consumer credit (97% outsourced to financial institutions) compared to trade credit (less than 3% transacted through the card system) has caused me to spend the past seven years trying to understand the differences in these two systems. It has also led to the creation of the FTRANS® payment system called Trade Credit Express™ that provides one of the alternatives for trade credit sellers to grow sales, as explained later in this chapter. (FTRANS has a patent pending on this system.)

The conclusion that I reached in researching this question is that bank credit cards have not captured a significant portion of trade credit because they disrupt a historical set of relationships in the trade credit process – a set of relationships that have developed over thousands of years. Parts of these relationships have been explained elsewhere in this book, but they are summarized here as follows:

1. Trade credit (accounts payable) is the largest source of capital for more businesses in the United States than any other source – it is a greater source for more businesses than bank loans and owners equity. Business buyers have apparently not been willing to give up this "free and flexible" source of capital in favor of the convenience and other benefits of using a credit card for making payments.

2. Trade credit buyers expect to control the time of payment, both to enforce seller performance and to manage their cash flow. The bank credit card system has rigid payment deadlines for the buyer.

3. Trade credit buyers expect trade credit to be free. The bank credit card system is not free for the buyer; it imposes interest and other charges on the buyer if payment is not made on a strict schedule.

4. The careful management of business customers, including the granting of trade credit and the exercise of flexible judgment in

setting terms and making collections, is critical for many trade credit sellers. The bank credit card system removes these functions from the seller's control.

In any purchasing transaction, the buyer generally controls the method of payment. The buyer may elect to pay with cash, by check, on a credit card, or to request trade credit. The relationships described in items #1 through #3 above are basically reasons that buyers require free and flexible trade credit and are not willing to make significant purchases on a credit card.

The relationship described in item #4 above is a seller decision and part of the reason that many trade credit sellers are reluctant to give up their internal credit system. Granting trade credit and being able to manage that process is critical to making sales and keeping customers.

What if you, a trade credit seller, could have the best of both worlds? What if you could outsource to financial institutions the headaches, risk, and funding of trade credit while not disrupting the historical requirements of trade credit (items #1 through #4 above)? The result is a system that would let you use longer payment terms and more flexible trade credit to grow sales, but have someone else take the risk of non-payment, fund the transactions, and have the business process burden. And, what if the outsourced system turns out to be less expensive than what you are currently spending in operating an internal trade credit system? It turns out that there are such outsourcing alternatives available, but each has limitations currently.

The first alternative, true factoring, has been available in the United States for at least 100 years, but it is generally available only for larger companies and in a limited set of industries. The second alternative, Trade Credit Express™ - an FTRANS® payment system - is available for trade credit sellers of any size and for a very wide set of industries, but it is currently available only in six southeastern states for most businesses. (There are a few exceptions to this geographic limitation, such as venture capital-backed companies, advertising agencies, trade associations, law firms, accounting firms, and broadcast stations. But, most companies will have to wait until late 2008 or 2009 or later to take advantage of this financial innovation.) The following two sections describe these two alternatives in detail.

"TRUE FACTORING"

I have used the adjective "true" and put the term "true factoring" in quotation marks to distinguish this financial service from receivables discounting or receivables financing, which is discussed in Chapter 9. True factoring is discussed in this Chapter 10 because it is a method of outsourcing business processes and risk, and is therefore a way of reducing the burden and funding of trade credit, rather than being a lending program. Or, said another way, true factoring is a method of reducing the use of capital and, therefore, relates to the output side of the Capital Flow Model, rather than being an input of capital on the left side.

In true factoring, the "factor" purchases the account from the seller without recourse. This means that the factor owns the account and the factor (not the seller) has the credit risk on the buyer. The factor also does the initial and ongoing credit evaluation, tracking, collections, etc. The factor will charge the seller a fee for the factoring services, which is normally a fixed percentage of the transaction volume. There may be some surcharges for longer payment terms, international customers, etc., but not for delayed payments by buyers. If requested by the seller, the factor may also make an advance of the payment and charge the seller interest on that advance until the factor collects the payment from the buyer or pays the seller from its own funds in the event the buyer has a financial inability to pay. The important thing to recognize is that the advance is only one component of the services provided by the true factor, where a loan is the primary service provided by the receivables discounter.

The credit card transaction is basically a "true factoring" transaction. The merchant sells the account to the issuing bank, which then has the credit risk on the buyer.

An interesting aspect of true factoring is that the accounting treatment for most transactions, under FASB Rule 140, would be to treat the advance as an early payment of the account, not a loan. For receivables discounting, asset based lending, or other forms of lending, an advance is recorded as a loan payable (a liability) by the seller. This favorable accounting treatment can have the effect of improving the balance sheet of the seller and reducing its debt to equity ratio among other benefits.

If a true factor can provide service to your businesses, it may be a very good way to fund the increased trade credit terms advocated by this book. In addition, many businesses find that outsourcing to financial institutions the risks and business processes of trade credit through true factoring is less expensive than operating an internal credit system.

I am a huge fan of true factoring. There are a few limitations, however. The three limitations that I have observed are:

1. One limitation is size of the seller. Since there has been considerable consolidation of the true factoring providers in recent years, there are only a few major players left in the industry and they have tended to move up market in recent years and serve only larger companies. The CIT Group / Commercial Services is the largest true factor in the United States. CIT tells me that their focus is businesses with $20 million in annual revenue and up, although I know of several cases where they have accepted smaller companies.

2. Another limitation of true factoring is industry focus. Although there are some differences among the true factors, they have traditionally been focused on certain core industries. For example, the focus of CIT appears to be industries related

to textiles, apparel, furniture, and home furnishings (and electronics on the west coast). That does not mean they will not serve other industries, but their expertise is clearly focused on their core. If you are a manufacturer or distributor in these industries with at least $20 million of annual sales, CIT is an excellent option.

3. The third limitation is standardization. One of the ways that traditional true factors are able to offer a cost effective service is to have a very high degree of standardization in the credit approval process, collections, etc. While this standardization seems to work well when most participants in a particular industry understand true factoring and know what to expect, it does not work as well in industries that do not have the same experience. For example, if you are in the supply chain for textiles in the United States, the chances are high that you have experience with true factoring and would not be surprised if CIT called to ask for credit information or make a collections call.

These three limitations may have kept true factoring from expanding beyond the traditional core industries and may have limited its ability to generally support the strategy advocated by this book. My informal tally of the annual volume of all the true factors in the United States indicates that their total volume is probably less than $200 billion of annual transactions – about 1% of trade credit sales, a number even smaller than trade credit sales through the bank credit card system.

FTRANS® TRADE CREDIT EXPRESS™

The second alternative for outsourcing the trade credit function and being able to fund the strategy advocated by this book is Trade Credit Express, a payment system from FTRANS.

As is clear from my biographical information, I have been personally and financially involved with the creation of FTRANS during the past five years. To paraphrase a former U.S. president introducing a book upon leaving the White House, in response to any charge that "this book is a boring and self-serving endorsement of FTRANS," I hope this book is not boring.

Trade Credit Express is a new financial innovation that was created in part to address the strategy advocated by this book. The initial motivation for creating Trade Credit Express was to give manufacturers and distributors the ability to grow sales by offering their retailers longer payment terms. (The background on this motivation is explained in more detail in Chapter 11, which explains the strategy as a tool to acquire other businesses.) But, it turns out that Trade Credit Express is more than just a tool to grow sales, it can be a significant part of an overall strategy to improve the operations and financial condition of a business.

Trade Credit Express has some of the characteristics of the bank credit card system, some characteristics of true factoring, and additional characteristics that are unique to Trade Credit Express.

Trade Credit Express enables B2B sellers to outsource to financial institutions the most difficult parts of their trade credit functions, while retaining control of the parts of trade credit that are critical to their business relationship with their customers. Trade Credit Express provides the opportunity to outsource all or part of the following three elements of the trade credit process:

- Business processes
- Credit risk on the buyer
- Funding

The outsourcing of these three elements is discussed in detail below.

Outsource the business processes related to trade credit

Trade Credit Express enables the business to outsource through FTRANS all or part of the following six business processes:

1. Obtaining and analyzing credit information on new business buyers (sellers may elect to participate in the collection of credit information from their buyers)

2. Monitoring the credit status of buyers on a continuous basis

3. Tracking accounts receivable after invoices have been sent to buyers

4. Receiving payments, matching payments to invoices, reconciling differences, and depositing payments in the bank

5. Performing collections for past due accounts (seller may elect to participate in the collections process)

6. Resolving disputes (cannot be entirely outsourced – seller must participate)

FTRANS and the financial institutions in its network are able to perform these business processes at a higher level of quality and for a lower cost than most individual businesses because they are performing them on a much larger scale, with better systems, and with expert personnel.

Outsource the buyer credit risk

In addition to the outsourcing of the business processes listed above, Trade Credit Express enables the B2B seller to outsource to financial institutions all or part of the risk associated with granting credit to the buyer. Financial institutions assume the risk that the buyer does not pay the account because of a financial inability to pay, including bankruptcy. This means that both the routine expense of bad debt and the potential risk of catastrophic failure of a major customer are covered by financial institutions.

This assumption of risk on the buyer does not cover the seller's failure to perform. If the buyer is refusing to pay due to a verified dispute with the seller, the burden falls back on the seller to resolve the dispute, just as it would without Trade Credit Express and as it would in accepting a credit card for payment. What the seller gains with Trade Credit Express is the involvement of a third party to help resolve the dispute.

In a similar fashion to disputes, the credit protection on the buyer does not cover fraudulent transactions by the seller. Just as with accepting a credit card for payment, if a seller puts a fraudulent invoice into the system (which is a violation of state and federal laws), the financial institution sponsoring the buyer is not liable when the buyer refuses to pay. The fraud and unresolved dispute risk remains with the seller, just as in the credit card system.

The financial institutions providing the credit risk protection on buyers through Trade Credit Express are able to deliver this service at a very reasonable cost because they are providing risk services on a huge volume of transactions, more than $300 billion annually in the United States and several times that amount globally. This economy of scale works for the benefit of the Trade Credit Express clients since they are obtaining the benefit of the credit protection spread over a huge portfolio. The Trade Credit Express client is not purchasing insurance from FTRANS, but they are receiving a similar benefit in a different legal form.

Outsource the funding of trade credit

The third component of trade credit that is outsourced to financial institutions through Trade Credit Express is the funding of the transaction. As in accepting a credit card for payment, Trade Credit Express causes the account receivable to be paid within a few days, rather than 30 or 60 days, or perhaps never. The participating bank that is making the advance payment to the seller is typically compensated by charging either (1) interest on the outstanding balance of the advance at a reasonable bank rate of interest, or (2) a fixed fee on the transaction that is adjusted from time to time based on changes in the bank's cost of capital and the average days sales outstanding on the accounts. The interest rates charged by the banks participating in

Trade Credit Express range from a low of about "LIBOR Plus 2.0%" to a high of about Prime Plus 4.0%, depending primarily on the annual volume of transactions and the credit worthiness of the seller. (See the Three Cs table below for more information on this point.) In a number of cases, the participating bank has lowered the rate they are charging a client that is now using Trade Credit Express since they judge their risk to be lower because the collateral is stronger and the capacity (cash flow) is assured. (The bank charge for the advance is in addition to the fee charged by FTRANS for the business process and risk outsourcing.)

As discussed above, the proper accounting treatment for advance payment of the invoice is typically booked by the seller as just that – early payment of the invoice, the same as accepting a credit card for payment. While the financial institution may show the advance as a loan on its books, it is typically not a loan on the books of the seller. Many banks participating in Trade Credit Express will require the seller to sign loan documents, but this is to protect the bank in the event that it has advanced funds on accounts that are fraudulent or have disputes that are resolved against the seller. The bank is looking to the financial institutions that are providing the credit protection on the buyer as the ultimate collateral on the accounts that are not fraudulent or have unresolved disputes.

Since the participating bank making the advances may be viewing the transaction as a loan on its books, it is useful to apply the Three Cs of lending to Trade Credit Express to see how the bank might view this relationship:

Summary of Three Cs – Applied to Trade Credit Express From the Bank's Point of View	
Capacity	The capacity to repay the advance with interest comes from the payments of the accounts by the buyers. This is similar to an asset-based loan secured with accounts receivable, but the difference is that the process is now being managed by financial institutions and not the individual seller. As a result, the participating bank has more visibility and less risk in making the advance.
Collateral	The secondary source of payment if the buyer cannot pay is the credit protection on the buyer provided by another financial institution. This credit protection is for the benefit of both the seller and the bank that is making the advance.
Character	The bank making the advance still must make a "character" decision on the seller since the credit protection that constitutes the "collateral" does not cover fraud or unresolved disputes. The bank must answer the question: "Can we trust the seller not to commit fraud and to be competent enough to keep the business operating so that it can resolve disputes in the ordinary course of business?"

Similarities with the Credit Card System

The bank credit card system has been fabulously successful, helping financial institutions now capture more than 97% of consumer credit. FTRANS designed Trade Credit Express to mimic as much as possible the positive attributes of the bank credit card system. As a result, Trade Credit Express has several similarities with the bank credit card system, including:

- Most of the business processes associated with operating a credit system are outsourced to financial institutions.

- Much of the risk of non-payment by the buyer is outsourced to a financial institution.

- Payments to the seller are made within a few days by a financial institution. When the seller receives the advance payment from the financial institution, the seller typically records the payment as early payment of the invoice, rather than as a loan from a financial institution.

- The entire process is highly automated with credit requests on buyers and settlement of transaction (assignments of invoices) made via a web-based system.

- The total cost to the seller of Trade Credit Express is about the same or less than the cost of accepting a credit card for payment.

- The risk to the financial institution sponsoring the seller (the bank making the advances) is that the seller enters fraudulent transitions or is unable to resolve disputes because it goes out of business (fraud and unresolved dispute risk, also called fraud and business continuity risk).

In using Trade Credit Express, the seller can elect to outsource almost all the trade credit functions to FTRANS, such that the interaction of the seller with Trade Credit Express is almost identical with that of a seller accepting a bank credit card for payment. However, the services of Trade Credit Express can also be purchased as components, which allow the seller to customize the service to their particular needs. These components are explained in the following section, Differences from the Credit Card System.

Differences from the Credit Card System

While the bank credit card system has been very successful in allowing consumer credit to be outsourced to financial institutions, it has failed to capture more than just 3% of trade credit transactions. Trade Credit Express has many similarities with the bank credit card system, but it has been designed specifically to overcome the conflicts that the bank credit card system has with the historical requirements of trade credit. As a result, there are important differences between Trade Credit Express and the bank credit card system. These differences include:

- In Trade Credit Express the seller pays the entire cost of the service and the buyer pays only the amount of the invoice. This is consistent with the historical tradition of free trade credit and is a requirement of most trade credit buyers. The requirement of the bank credit card system that buyers pay interest or other fees is one of the reasons why the bank credit card has failed to gain significant penetration in trade credit.

- In Trade Credit Express the buyer controls the timing of the payment, also a historical requirement of trade credit. There is no financial penalty if the buyer is late in making the payment. If the buyer is significantly or habitually late, or defaults on the payment entirely, their credit rating will be adversely impacted. If the payment is several months past due, the buyer may face a serious collection effort, including legal action at the expense of the financial institution that sponsored the buyer.

- In Trade Credit Express the business buyer does not have to consent to participating in the system or having their credit checked, unlike the bank credit card system in which the consumer must consent to their credit being checked and being issued a card and participating in the system. With trade credit in general, and Trade Credit Express specifically, the business buyer is automatically in the system when they accept the offer of trade credit from the seller. In Trade Credit Express, the business buyer does not have a card and does not need to present an account number to have their business credit checked or their account receivable (represented by an invoice) assigned to a financial institution. The seller enters their business buyers into the system by entering the business name, address, and telephone number, which is usually sufficient to identify the business and secure credit approval. [The two notable exceptions to the general rule of not having to secure the consent of the buyer for participation are with (1) the federal government where the Assignment of Claims Act requires that the consent of the contracting officer be secured, which usually can be accomplished, and (2) business clients of law firms where the client must consent in order to conform to requirements of the ethics rules as adopted in most jurisdictions.)

- With Trade Credit Express there is more flexibility available on where the payments go and to whom checks are made payable. In the bank credit card system, payments are payable and addressed to the financial institution sponsoring the buyer. In Trade Credit Express the payments are payable to the seller and are usually sent to a post office box in the seller's home state.

- With Trade Credit Express, there is more flexibility in the collections activity than with a bank credit card where past due amounts are collected by the financial institution sponsoring the buyer. With trade credit, many sellers want to have an active role in the management of the collections process since their relationship with their buyers is one of the most important assets of their business. In Trade Credit Express, the seller can elect to have an active role in collections or not. In some cases, the seller is happy to be removed from the collections process entirely. In other cases, sellers want varying levels of involvement, at least for certain important buyers.

Industry and Other Limitations of Trade Credit Express

Trade Credit Express has been designed to serve a wide variety of trade credit sellers in the United States, but it is not a universal program. The type of businesses that can be served by Trade Credit Express cover the range of industries from extraction of raw materials, to manufacturing, wholesale distribution, contracting, and professional services. The only major business categories not served by Trade Credit Express are those retail establishments that sell to businesses only on credit cards. If the retail establishment has an internal trade credit function today, or could increase sales by offering trade credit to business customers, then Trade Credit Express might be applicable.

There are some situations in which Trade Credit Express does not work very well. These include:

- Progress billing, such as might be performed by a general contractor, because of the uncertainty of what is due and the potential for disputes. Sub-contractors that are billing for specific work completed do perform well in the Trade Credit Express system.

- Billings where the underlying claims relate to consumer health care. Even though a physician may be billing an insurance company, the underlying claim is for consumer medical services. The limitation here is the high level of disputes that routinely occur in these transactions.

- Where the credit of the buyers is weak. FTRANS has had a few clients that were selling to buyers in distressed industries and it was difficult to get the buyers approved for credit by financial institutions. Early on, one client selling to airlines had this problem, but this industry has largely recovered and the problem has abated somewhat. Another client selling medical products had difficulty getting nursing homes and home health care agencies approved. FTRANS expects that it will become more difficult to get general contractors approved in the coming months as the construction industry continues to suffer from the downturn in housing.

- Where the credit of the seller is very weak. Since a financial institution must sponsor the seller and assume the fraud and unresolved dispute risk on the seller, it is difficult for a seller with really bad credit to be approved. Many of the usual limitations of approving a seller for a traditional commercial line of credit do not apply with Trade Credit Express, such as age of the business, years of profitability, etc. But, bad credit on the part of the business or the owners can be a limitation.

Geographic Limitations of Trade Credit Express

In addition to the industry and other limitations of Trade Credit Express discussed in the previous section, there are also currently geographic limitations. With the exception of the six industries listed below, at the time this book was written, Trade Credit Express is only available to the full range of trade credit sellers in the six southeastern states of Alabama, Florida, Georgia, North Carolina, South Carolina, and Tennessee (and metro-areas on the edge of these states, such as Memphis). This geographic limitation is a result of FTRANS having started Trade Credit Express in the southeast and having recruited seller-sponsor banks only in these six states. FTRANS plans to expand Trade Credit Express into other regions in 2008 and by the time you read this book, FTRANS may have added additional states. Check the FTRANS website, found in Appendix B, for a list of states served.

Although FTRANS is able to offer coverage for trade credit buyers in 100 countries, it is able to offer national coverage only for sellers in six specific industries since it has financial institutions willing to participate in the sponsorship of sellers in these categories. National coverage is currently available for:

- Venture-backed companies: firms with recognized venture capital investors

- Advertising agencies

- Trade associations

- Radio and television stations

- Law firms (may require state bar approval of Trade Credit Express as conforming to client confidentiality and other client billing and fee requirements)

- Accounting firms (also may require state approval of Trade Credit Express as conforming to client confidentiality and other client billing and fee requirements)

CONCLUSION

The two methods of increasing the ability to grant trade credit by outsourcing trade credit functions described in this chapter can be the key ingredient for executing the core strategy advocated by this book: using the credit crisis to grow your B2B business. These two methods also have application for another way to grow a business – through acquisitions. That strategy is covered in Chapter 11.

USE OF TRADE CREDIT TO ACQUIRE OTHER COMPANIES

How to use trade credit as a primary mechanism to fund acquisitions or buy out a partner.

The first 10 chapters of this book describe how to grow sales by granting customers more trade credit on more flexible terms. This chapter discusses another way to grow a business – by using trade credit to acquire other businesses. The strategy outlined in this chapter also applies to a related financial strategy – buying out a partner.

TRADE CREDIT AS AN ACQUISITION TOOL

I first became aware of the significant proactive power of trade credit in the late 1990s when building a company that was consolidating sales agencies in the home furnishing industry. During a two year period, we purchased 23 sales agencies, which resulted in a company with more than 350 sales people and more than $600 million in sales for the 600 manufacturers the agencies represented.

This consolidation was accomplished in part by using trade credit to acquire the target companies. The financial strategy was straight-forward:

- Buy the target sales agency for about 4 times operating income and pay 25% in cash, and have the seller finance the balance after subtracting any significant debt to be assumed.

- Use the accounts receivables of the acquired agency as collateral for an asset-based loan to cover 50% or more of the cash portion of the purchase price.

The actual financial model for each acquisition was fairly complicated, but a simple pro-forma summary of this strategy illustrates how it worked:

Sales by agency for manufacturers	$10,000,000
Commission rate earned by sales agency	10%
= Commission revenue for sales agency	**$1,000,000**
Less cost of sales agents	$600,000
Less other operating costs	$200,000
= Operating income of agency	**$200,000**
Purchase price of agency (4X operating income)	$800,000
Purchase price paid in cash ("down payment" of 25%)	$200,000
Accounts receivable (60 days of commission revenue)	$166,000
Funding on A/R (80% of A/R)	$133,000
Net cash required ($200,000 - $133,000)	$67,000
Net cash required as a % of down payment	**33%**
Net cash required as a % of purchase price	**8%**

This example indicates it is possible to reduce the upfront cash required by two-thirds by using the capital available through funding on the accounts receivable. In addition, there was one more piece of financial engineering applied:

Reduction in back office cost	$40,000
First year operating income plus reduction in back office cost ($200,000 + $40,000)	$240,000
First year operating income plus reduction in back office cost – per month ($240,000 / 12)	$20,000
Number of months required to earn back net cash investment ($67,000 / $20,000)	**3.3 months**

The financial details of the actual transactions were, of course, more complicated than the simple example given above. However, this example does illustrate that it took a relatively short period of time to earn back the capital required to make the acquisitions.

It is not always possible to have the seller finance part of the sale. We were fortunate that many of the sellers of the agencies were willing to take a note for the purchase price. In some cases they were interested in selling in order to retire and they saw a note from a larger organization as being preferable to their other alternatives. The fact that we were willing to pay typically 4 times operating income was attractive. This amount, as in the example above, was equal to about four years of expected earnings. This meant that the seller received an upfront cash payment equal to about what they would have earned over the next 12 months, assuming they had no bumps in the business. Plus, they had the assurance of monthly payments for the next three years thereafter that were higher than they would have earned in the business. Also, we frequently paid interest only for a short period of time, 6 months or so, and in some cases we were able to negotiate a deferral of any payments for 6 months with the interest accruing, and then arranged for a 36 month payout.

Leveraging the A/R in these acquisitions significantly reduced the capital required. The first two agencies we acquired were with equity exchanges or all cash secured by selling equity. Those two agencies had combined annual commission revenue of about $5 million; leveraging their A/R produced enough cash to purchase an additional group of agencies with about the same total commission revenue.

The example above of using the A/R to help make acquisitions is not new for large scale transactions – it has been in the toolkit of mergers and acquisition specialists for many years. But, it can now be used in smaller transactions by applying any of the sources of obtaining capital described in Chapters 9 and 10.

TRADE CREDIT TO BUYOUT A PARTNER

Converting the investment currently being made in trade credit (accounts receivable) to cash can be useful in another acquisition scenario, the buy-out of a shareholder or partner. Example 5 in Chapter 12 provides the details on how this was applied in structuring a buy-out of a partner in an engineering firm.

The key in that example is that the engineering firm had a large amount of outstanding trade credit due to the fact that most of its clients were slow-paying government agencies.

Not every case has a fact situation that permits the accounts receivable to be used in this manner. For example, the fact situation outlined in Example 4 in Chapter 12 is one such case – there is just too much debt secured by accounts to provide the owner any leeway.

EXAMPLES OF USE IN SPECIFIC INDUSTRIES

Examples in manufacturing, wholesale distribution, staffing, and professional services.

The examples illustrated in this chapter are presented to help you understand how to apply the strategy advocated by this book of using expanded trade credit to grow sales. These examples are taken from actual situations and present the alternatives that each company faced. In each case, the starting numbers are changed to reflect averages for each category of capital for that particular industry or for a representative national company in order to make the examples relevant for the widest possible audience. The annual revenue for each example has been normalized to $10 million to facilitate comparisons to other businesses.

Each example provides a current financial overview, explains the specific opportunity, and analyzes the available alternatives.

EXAMPLE 1: MANUFACTURER OF POLLUTION CONTROL EQUIPMENT

Herman Punch owns a Tampa-based manufacturer of pollution control equipment used in a variety of other manufacturing plants. Major customers have been stretching out payments recently to a DSO of nearly 90 days and several have advised Herman to expect even longer payment times in coming months. Customers range from other middle-size companies to the largest manufacturers in the United States. The business has been growing since it was founded in 1998, but growth has been irregular as new, large customers have been added. The business had been only marginally profitable, but now appears that it can produce a good operating margin when sales are over about $9 million annually. Herman has provided all of the equity to date, initially from savings and more recently from a home equity line of credit on his house. Herman owns 100% of the company. The business saw a rapid decline in late 2001 following September 11, 2001 and suffered losses in 2002 through 2005, which created a deficit in net worth that was overcome in 2006.

The financial statements for 2007 show:

Financial Measure	Dollars	% of Sales	DSO
Cash	71,856	0.72%	2.62
Accounts Receivable	2,428,084	24.3%	88.6
Inventory	1,359,776	13.6%	49.6
PP&E	2,149,677	21.5%	78.5
Other Assets	88,059	0.88%	3.21
Accounts Payable	1,986,364	19.9%	72.5
Bank Debt	3,502,503	35.0%	128
Other Liabilities	532,747	5.33%	19.4
Equity	75,838	0.76%	2.77
Revenue	10,000,000	100.0%	365
COGS	7,908,846	79.1%	289
Gross Profit	2,091,154	20.9%	76.3
Bad Debt	35,742	0.36%	1.3
Other Operating Expense	1,530,800	15.3%	55.9
Operating Income	524,612	5.25%	19.1

Herman approached his local bank where he has maintained the business and his personal accounts since the inception of the business. This bank had provided a loan on the building and equipment of just over $2 million and a line of credit of $1,500,000 million, loosely secured with a lien on inventory and accounts receivable and Herman's personal guaranty. The interest rate on the line of credit was at Prime plus 1.0%.

Herman asked the bank to increase his line of credit by $500,000, in order to be able to fund the increased accounts receivable he expects as his major customers slow their payments. The bank did not feel comfortable with their current position under their newly adopted, more restrictive lending policies, despite a 10 year history with Herman. In particular, the bank was uncomfortable with the small amount of equity and the fact the business had been unprofitable for three of the past five years. The banker told Herman he needed to seek alternative funding for any increase in the line of credit and the bank would really prefer that Herman to take the line elsewhere. They were happy to keep the real estate loan, at least for now.

However, the banker helped Herman review his situation and made several recommendations. First, Herman's inventory level at the end of 2007 was 17% of cost of goods sold, or 63 days turn, exactly the industry average for fabricated metal products manufactures (two-digit SIC code 34). Herman's accounts payable was 25% of cost of goods sold, or a DPO (Days Payables Outstanding) of 90 days, also exactly the industry average. The banker suggested four possible courses of action:

1. Ask customers to pay faster or stop selling to those who took more than 60 days to pay. (This advice was a non-starter for Herman, since most of his customer took more than 60 days to pay and if he demanded faster payment, he was afraid he would lose the customers.)

2. Ask suppliers for more time – increasing the average accounts payable time from 90 days by only 15 more days would add more than $330,000 available cash. (Herman tried this approach, but without any significant improvement in terms. Most of his suppliers were already giving him 90 days, and would not go longer.)

3. Approach another bank in town that offered an asset-based lending (ABL) program. If his business qualified, the banker told Herman this would be less expensive than receivables discounting.

4.   Approach a non-bank receivables discounting company to which the bank frequently made referrals. The banker told Herman this might be more expensive, but it was likely he could get the money he needed.

Herman initially approached the bank that offered the ABL program. At first, it looked promising, despite the fact that the line Herman sought was on the low end of what the bank preferred for an ABL line. Herman spent three weeks assembling all the information the bank requested. The bank offered Herman an ABL line with the following formula:

- $2,500,000 maximum line, origination fee of 1.0% of line at closing ($25,000) plus closing costs of about 0.6% ($15,000). Prime plus 2% interest, plus quarterly audit and analysis fees of about $5,000 per quarter.

- 75% loan on "eligible" accounts receivable and 40% loan on inventory (down from the bank's usual 50% on inventory due to their tightening standards).

Herman calculated that he would be advanced $2,365,000 under the formula, $1,821,000 on 75% of the A/R at the end of 2007 and $544,000 on 40% of the inventory. This was $865,000 more than his current line and sufficient for his estimated needs. His interest cost would go up by about $30,000 on the base of the current $1,500,000 line, his cost for the audits would add about $20,000 more annually. The initial cost of the loan was an additional $40,000, for a total of $90,000 extra cost in the first year. With a gross margin of nearly 21%, Herman calculated that his sales would have to go up by nearly $430,000 to cover this additional cost. Since he felt that having some flexibility with his current customers would add at least a 5% increase in sales ($500,000) and gross profit ($105,000), and probably more, the $90,000 of additional cost was worth it.

Herman took the package to his accountant to review before closing. The accountant pointed out that the bank's definition of "eligible" accounts receivable disallowed all amounts due from customers when any invoice was over 60 days past due or over 90 days from date of invoice (cross-aging). Since about 40% of Herman's accounts receivable were with customers in one of these categories, the actual availability on accounts receivable was about 45% (60% times 75%), and instead of the 75% that Herman had calculated. This lowered the availability under the formula to about $1,636,000, only $136,000 more than his current line and far short of his need. Herman asked the ABL group to relax this requirement; they declined.

Herman then approached the receivables discounting company. Since Herman had already assembled the package for the bank ABL group, he was able to get a quick decision. The receivables discounter offered:

- $2,000,000 million line, 80% loan on accounts receivable, no loan on inventory, any invoice over 91 days past due (91 days beyond Net 30 Days) or 121 days after the invoice date would be ineligible (charged back).

- The discount charges would be based on the face amount of the invoice (not the amount loaned): 2.0% for the first 30 days and 1.5% for each 30 days period thereafter, or any factional part of 30 days. In addition, interest would be paid at 6.0% on the outstanding loan. There was a 2.0% closing fee ($40,000).

Herman took this package to his accountant, who analyzed the payment history of Herman's customers and determined that almost exactly 50% paid between the 61 and 90 days (incurring a charge of 5.0% on the face account of transactions) and 40% paid between 91 and 120 days (incurring a charge of 6.5% on the face amount), and 10% were paying beyond 120 days. For this final 10% Herman would be charged an 8.0% fee and then the principal amount charged back to Herman. The accountant calculated that Herman's cost for this alternative, had he been using it in 2007, would have been $590,000 in discount fees plus $115,000 in interest, or about $570,000 more than

Herman had paid the bank in interest in 2007 and 86% of Herman's operating income in 2007. Herman calculated that, with a gross margin of 21%, his sales would have to increase by $2.7 million, or a 27% increase over 2007, to cover these increased costs.

Then the accountant suggested that Herman check with another bank in town that was now offering FTRANS Trade Credit Express. Since Herman was now very well equipped with the right information, he got a quick proposal from the new bank:

- Outsource the trade credit function to FTRANS at a cost of 1.0% of the face amount of the transactions, and FTRANS would assume the credit approval functions, risk of non-payment by customers, tracking, collections, matching payments to invoices, and operating a lock-box.

- The bank would make advance payment equal to 90% of invoices to FTRANS approved customers with a cap of $2,500,000 initially, but the cap could rise as the trade credit sales increased. The bank would charge 1.0% ($25,000) to establish the line and charge Prime Plus 1.5% of the amount advanced.

Herman took this package to his accountant who calculated that the cost of the internal functions that would be outsourced to FTRANS currently cost Herman approximately $50,000 in addition to $35,000 of bad debt in 2007, for a total internal cost of about $85,000 that would be eliminated. The FTRANS proposal was for 1.0%, or $100,000 at the 2007 sales volume. Herman was concerned that his bad-debt expense and internal costs of collections might go up in 2008 as the economy declined and his major customers faced more financial pressure. Herman concluded the cost of the FTRANS fee was about equal to what his internal costs would be in 2008. The FTRANS program also relieved a significant headache and risk from the business.

The issue then was whether the bank's 90% advance payment would be sufficient since it applied only to FTRANS approved customers. Herman submitted his customer list to FTRANS, which determined that it could initially approve customers representing about 90% of Herman's annual sales in 2007. Herman and his accountant calculated that his eligible accounts receivable would have been $1,967,000 (90% times 90% outstanding A/R) at the end of 2007, slightly below Herman's target. The bank's cost of this loan would be 0.5% above his old line, or $7,500 on the 2007 end of year number, in addition to the $25,000 in origination and closing fees. Herman calculated his sales would have to increase by 1.6% ($160,000) to cover this additional $32,500 first year cost. Herman decided that the peace of mind of not having to worry about the potential failure of a major customer adversely impacting his business was worth the $32,500 of additional cost, even if there were no additional sales.

Herman's accountant also concluded that, under FASB Rule 140, the early payment of invoices under the FTRANS program would not be reported as debt on the balance sheet, thereby improving Herman's debt to equity ratio.

EXAMPLE 2: IMPORTER AND WHOLESALE DISTRIBUTOR OF FURNITURE

Wendy Divan started her company in Dallas in 1993 to import furniture from Asia and distribute it to small and midsize furniture retailers throughout the United States. She built the business over a 15 year period and reached $10 million in sales in 2007. At first, her gross margins were better than 40%, with cost of sales less than 60%, including freight to bring the product into the United States and the 10% sales commission she paid independent sales agencies. Wendy typically gives net 30 day payment terms and her customers pay on average in 46 days.

Wendy started the business by making the initial inventory purchases on her personal credit card and a small loan from a friend. She built the equity in the company to more than $1 million by mid-2001 by leaving most of the earnings in the company. Wendy was able to persuade the suppliers of about half of her inventory to give her net 30 day terms; the other half she had to pay as the goods shipped from Asia. In 1999, Wendy bought the warehouse she was using with a $1,000,000 SBA guaranteed loan that has been paid down to under $750,000.

Following the impact of September 11th, Wendy suffered setbacks in late 2001 and 2002 that wiped out half her equity. Her sales recovered in late 2003 and beyond and her equity has been built to $1.4 million at the end of 2007. She obtained a $250,000 line of credit from a community bank in 2005 based on her personal credit score, for which she paid about $20,000 in interest in 2007. During the past two years, her margins have been eroding with increased competition on price, higher inbound freight charges, and the sales agencies insisting on 12% commission.

For 2007, the financial statements for Wendy's business are as follows:

Financial Measure	Dollars	% of Sales	DSO
Cash	235,225	2.35%	8.59
Accounts Receivable	1,245,744	12.5%	45.5
Inventory	485,144	4.85%	17.7
PP&E	893,092	8.93%	32.6
Other Assets	96,265	0.96%	3.51
Accounts Payable	355,649	3.56%	13
Bank Debt	958,151	9.58%	35
Other Liabilities	233,611	2.34%	8.53
Equity	1,408,059	14.1%	51.4
Revenue	10,000,000	100%	365
COGS	8,248,306	82.5%	301
Gross Profit	1,751,694	17.5%	63.9
Bad Debt	36,000	0.36%	1.31
Other Operating Expense	1,236,923	12.4%	45.1
Operating Income	478,771	4.79%	17.5

In late 2007, Wendy called her top 50 customers to ask what she could do to serve them better. There were a number of suggestions, but the one consistent theme was to give payment terms longer than just 30 days. In order to find the capital to offer longer terms to her customers, she asked her suppliers for longer terms. The suppliers currently giving her net 30 and the ones requiring immediate payment told her the same thing: give us a bank letter of credit to receive longer terms. The largest supplier currently giving her net 30 day terms told Wendy that he would have to discontinue entirely the practice of giving terms if the global credit crisis did not abate soon; he also told her to expect to have to pay for her next order at the time it shipped, approximately $200,000, which would exhaust most of her cash.

Wendy approached the bank that she had been using since opening the business in 1993. At that time, the bank was a local community bank. It was acquired by a regional bank in 1997, which in turn was acquired by a multi-regional bank in 1999. The banker who opened Wendy's original account and made the SBA loan in 1999 left in 2001 to join another community bank. Wendy used that banker and her community bank for the $250,000 line in 2005. At the multi-regional bank, Wendy was directed to a business banking specialist who told Wendy that the bank no longer issued letters of credit and had no program to provide working capital financing for a business her size. The bank recommended either obtaining a line of credit on her personal credit or applying for another SBA loan, also on her personal credit, to replace the current SBA loan.

Wendy approached her banker at the community bank where she had the $250,000 line. The banker told Wendy they did not have a credit program for funding accounts receivable, but they did work with a regional bank that had an ABL (asset based loan) department. After checking, Wendy learned the minimum line for the ABL group is $3 million, and she would not qualify.

The banker then told Wendy that she had read about Trade Credit Express and suggested that Wendy contact FTRANS, who told Wendy they were sorry, but they only covered her industry type in the southeast. (At the time this book was written, the national coverage of FTRANS is limited to venture-backed companies, advertising agencies, law firms, accounting firms, trade associations, and broadcast stations.)

The local banker then referred Wendy to a receivables financing company, which quoted the following:

- $1,500,000 million line, 80% loan on accounts receivable, no loan on inventory, any invoice over 91 days past due would be ineligible (charged back).

- The discount charges would be based on the face amount of the invoice (not the amount loaned): 2.0% for the first 30 days and each 30 day period thereafter, or any factional part of 30 days. In addition, interest would be paid at 8.0% on the outstanding loan. There would be a 1.5% closing fee ($22,500), plus a monthly analysis fee of $1,000.

Wendy and her accountant analyzed the proposal from the receivables discounter and determined that for 2007, 10% of invoices were paid in less than 30 days, 60% in 30 to 60 days, 20% in 60 to 90 days, and 10% in more than 90 days. The total discount charge for this distribution of payments would be $460,000 on $10 million of sales, plus $12,000 for the monthly analysis fee, and about $80,000 of interest on an average of $1,000,000 outstanding. This would result in increased costs of more than $552,000, or 115% of Wendy's operating income in 2007. At her current gross profit of 17.5%, Wendy would have to increase her annual sales by more than $3,150,000, or 31.5%, to cover the $552,000 of additional cost. Despite the fact that Wendy thought she could grow sales by offering more credit to her customers, the 31.5% step to break even was too high.

Wendy elected not to use the receivables discounter, but was able to increase her $250,000 loan with the community bank to $350,000, not sufficient to fully cover the increased need to pay the Asian supplier at time of shipment and not sufficient to offer her customers increased payment terms, but enough to get her through the tight spot.

EXAMPLE 3: IMPORTER AND WHOLESALE DISTRIBUTOR OF HOME ACCESSORIES

Sally Stuph started her company in Atlanta in the mid-1990s and has been a friend of Wendy Divan (Example 2) since they met at the Dallas market in 1996. Sally imports home products from Asia and distributes them to small and midsize furniture and home accessory retailers throughout the United States. She built the business over a 12 year period and reached $10 million in sales in 2007.

The financial statements for Sally's business for 2007 are:

Financial Measure	Dollars	% of Sales	DSO
Cash	193,589	1.94%	7.07
Accounts Receivable	1,866,284	18.7%	68.1
Inventory	267,772	2.68%	9.77
PP&E	53,975	0.54%	1.97
Other Assets	104,453	1.04%	3.81
Accounts Payable	351,300	3.51%	12.8
Bank Debt	790,019	7.9%	28.8
Other Liabilities	359,838	3.6%	13.1
Equity	984,916	9.85%	35.9
Revenue	10,000,000	100%	365
COGS	6,490,476	64.9%	237
Gross Profit	3,509,524	35.1%	128
Bad Debt	92,500	0.93%	3.38
Other Operating Expense	3,095,462	31%	113
Operating Income	321,562	3.22%	11.7

There are many similarities in Sally's and Wendy's businesses – they both exhibit at the major markets (Atlanta, Dallas, New York, Chicago, and San Francisco), use outside sales agencies as their sale forces, and sell to the same type of retailers.

However, there are major differences between the businesses. First, the gross margin that Sally is able to obtain (35%) is twice what Wendy can earn, primarily due to the willingness of retailers to buy the unique products Sally offers and generally lower price point of each item. Sally's standard wholesale pricing target is to obtain the "keystone markup" by multiplying her landed cost by 2. She pays the sales agencies 12% to 15% of the sales price, resulting in a Cost of Goods Sold of about 65%. Sally has been able to obtain 2% 10 - Net 30 day terms from three of her major suppliers; she takes the full 30 days to pay. The other suppliers are paid when the goods are shipped from Asia.

Second, she has been giving the retailers Net 45 or Net 60 day pricing for years, in order to encourage larger orders and increase sales. Sally's standard terms are Net 30 for orders under $500, Net 45 for orders between $500 and $1,000, and Net 60 for orders over $1,000. She was encouraged to use this formula by one of her sales agencies in the late 1990s and discovered that it did increase sales.

Sally has been funding the increased receivables with a receivables discounting firm that is charging her 2.0% for each 30 day period the invoice is outstanding and no other charges. Invoices over 61 days past due or 91 days from invoice date are not eligible for borrowing. In 2007, she paid the discounter $520,000 in fees, or 5.2% of her sales and about 28% of the average outstanding accounts receivable. Sally knows the $520,000 is expensive, but she justifies it on the basis that offering longer payment terms has allowed her to double her sales over the past six years and the margin on the additional $5,000,000 in sales is about $1,750,000, for a net gain of about $1,230,000.

Wendy told Sally about her research on sources of additional capital and Sally decided to see if she could improve her situation. Sally approached her bank in Atlanta and learned they offer the FTRANS Trade Credit Express program. The bank and FTRANS helped Sally conduct an analysis of her current internal credit functions. The bank proposed an advance payment of 85% of the invoices to approved customers under the FTRANS program, with a cap of $1,500,000, at an interest rate of Prime Plus 2.0% (8.0% total at the time) for a total annual cost of $120,000, if Sally took the maximum advance. FTRANS proposed a fee of 1.25% for the trade credit outsourcing functions, including covering 90% of the risk of non-payment by Sally's customers, for a total annual cost of $125,000 at $10 million in sales. The total of the bank and FTRANS charges would be about $245,000.

Sally determined that with the FTRANS program she could eliminate about $90,000 in bad debt, $30,000 in back-office expenses, and save about $60,000 with early pay discounts with vendors, for a total savings of $180,000, leaving the net cost of the bank and FTRANS program at $65,000, a $455,000 savings compared to the current cost of the discounter of $520,000. She also realized that she was reducing the burden of operating an internal credit system, eliminating the risk of a default by a large customer, and gaining a tool to further increase sales, thereby implementing the strategy advocated by this book.

EXAMPLE 4: SECURITY STAFFING COMPANY

George Harris is the 100% owner of Harris Services, a temporary staffing company in Columbia that supplies maintenance workers for local governments and regional airports. He started the company in 1996, after being employed by one of the major airlines for 20 years. George's business is much like other staffing companies, large and small, with more than 80% of his revenue payable to the employees and for benefits. He must pay his employees every two weeks, but finds that his customers take an average of 80 days to pay him. Part of the issue is that he is actually a subcontractor (for about 60% of his revenue) with a winning bidder between George's company and the local government, airport authority, or airline actually paying the bills.

Financial Measure	Dollars	% of Sales	DSO
Cash	191,687	1.92%	7
Accounts Receivable	2,184,883	21.8%	79.7
Inventory	-	-	-
PP&E	115,075	1.15%	4.2
Other Assets	17,452	0.17%	0.64
Accounts Payable	56,705	0.57%	2.07
Bank Debt	2,450,505	24.5%	89.4
Other Liabilities	93,089	0.93%	3.4
Equity	(91,203)	(0.91%)	(3.33)
Revenue	10,000,000	100%	365
COGS	8,208,683	82.1%	300
Gross Profit	1,791,317	17.9%	65.4
Bad Debt	120,000	1.2%	4.38
Other Operating Expense	1,686,761	16.9%	61.6
Operating Income	(15,445)	(0.15)	(0.56)

Following the crisis in the airline industry after September 11th, George's business almost failed. The airlines delayed payment of their invoices and George had an immediate cash crisis. He was rescued by Morning Glory Services (MGS), a firm that provides payroll processing and bookkeeping services for temporary staffing firms. MGS offered to loan George the $300,000 to cover his immediate payroll need, and to pay the payroll and other expenses going forward and collect the receivables for a fee of 5.0% of billings, plus 10% annual interest on the amount advanced, until paid by the customers. MGS was not assuming any credit risk on the customers, but would keep the A/R on the books for several months before they charged it back to George. MGS is essentially a type of receivable discounter, but one that provides additional payroll and accounting services for a specific vertical market.

In 2007, George paid MGS more than $720,000 in fees and interest, 7.2% of sales and more than 40% of his gross profit. In addition, he had a bad debt expense of $120,000 due to the failure of a contractor with whom he had a subcontract for a county government. George realized that he could outsource the payroll and accounting services being performed by MGS for a few thousand dollars annually by using ADP or another business process outsourcing firm. However, he needed to find a way to pay off the approximately $2,370,000 that he owed MGS in order to terminate the arrangement. MGS holds a first position security interest in all assets of George's business.

George has an $80,000 home equity line of credit with a large, multi-regional bank; George invested the entire amount in the company (it is included in the company's balance sheet). He approached that bank and several others about a loan to replace the MGS debt. All the banks turn him down, primarily due to the fact that the business has no equity and has lost money for the past six years. George explained to the banks that he would make more than $200,000 in profit if he could replace MGS, and found a sympathetic banker at a community bank. However, since the MGS line was more than 108% of the A/R and the bank's policy was not to advance on more than 75% on A/R, there is a large gap. The banker told George that he needed to find $750,000 in equity to close the gap.

George talked to several other owners of staffing companies for suggestions on an equity investor, but was not able to identify any prospects. One of the other staffing companies told George about FTRANS Trade Credit Express. George contacted FTRANS who worked with a local community bank to analyze the situation. FTRANS proposed a fee of 1.25% ($125,000) on transaction volume. The local bank was willing to advance George 90% of the A/R on FTRANS approved customers at an interest charge of Prime Plus 2%. For 2007, the bank and FTRANS fees would have been about $270,000 or $450,000 less than the fees charged by MGS.

However, the bank's 90% advance would fall about $380,000 short of paying off MGS, which MGS required to release their first position security interest in the A/R and other assets. George asked the bank to make an unsecured loan of the $380,000, which would be repaid from the first year savings in the MGS arrangement. The bank agreed, provided that George could provide security for the $380,000, which at this point George has been unable to do – there is not sufficient equity in his home and he owns no other real estate. At the moment, George is still looking for a way to close that gap.

EXAMPLE 5:   ENGINEERING SERVICES COMPANY

Jack Bridger and his partner, Mike Spanner, have owned Spanner & Bridger, Inc., (S&B) a civil engineering firm in Jacksonville for more than 15 years. Both Jack and Mike worked for the Florida Department of Transportation as engineers before starting their firm. S&B does civil engineering design work, primarily bridge work for state departments of transportation. The states take a long time to pay invoices, primarily because once an invoice is submitted it must be approved by several units of each state DOT before it is paid.

S&B has grown to $10 million in annual revenue in 2007 and its accounts receivable have grown to $2.8 million at the same time. S&B has been able to fund this high level of trade credit (reactive trade credit, since to perform the state work the firm must endure the long payment cycle) through accumulated earnings over the years, and a $1,000,000 term loan made in 2004 that has been reduced to $548,000. In addition, S&B pays its employees at the end of the month following the month the firm invoices clients, a practice initiated when the firm was created, which has produced $733,000 in accounts payable. Jack and Mike each personally guaranteed the $1,000,000 term loan, which is also secured with a pledge of all assets of the firm.

The financials for 2007 are:

Financial Measure	Dollars	% of Sales	DSO
Cash	723,807	7.24%	26.4
Accounts Receivable	2,808,600	28.1%	103
Inventory	-	-	-
PP&E	227,153	2.27%	8.29
Other Assets	240,243	2.4%	8.77
Accounts Payable	733,976	7.34%	26.8
Bank Debt	548,359	5.48%	20
Other Liabilities	514,792	5.42%	19.8
Equity	2,175,677	21.8%	79.4
Revenue	10,000,000	100%	365
COGS	8,570,506	85.7%	313
Gross Profit	1,429,494	14.3%	52.2
Bad Debt	-	-	-
Other Operating Expense	342,253	3.42%	12.5
Operating Income	1,087,241	10.9%	39.7

Jack and Mike are equal owners and each earns about $500,000 a year
from the firm (essentially splitting the operating income.) Mike wants
to retire and Jack would like to buy him out. They have struggled
over the price for nearly a year, with Mike contending the value of the
business should be equated to that of publically listed engineering
firms, with a value ranging from about 1.0 times revenue ($10 million)
to 15 times EBITDA (operating income), or about $16.3 million.
Jack's advisors have asserted that a privately owned engineering firm
cannot be valued by the same metrics as a publically listed firm, and
Mike has finally agreed to settle for a valuation on the firm of about 6
times operating income, or $6.5 million as of December 31, 2007. He
has also agreed to accept a note payable over three years for $750,000
of the $3.25 million purchase price for his 50% of the equity, provided

that his personal guarantee on the term loan is released. Jack needs to find the $2.5 million to make the purchase.

The bank that the firm has used for over ten years had made the term loan and is has been a very active user of the FTRANS payment system. The bank agreed to advance 90% of the accounts receivable processed through FTRANS, which would immediately provide the $2.5 million. The $500,000 portion of the operating income, after taxes, that will now be available can easily fund the three year amortization of the $750,000 portion of the purchase price.

NEXT STEPS: A ROAD MAP FOR GROWTH

How to implement the strategy. A recommended ranking of the alternatives for funding.

This book describes an overall strategy of growing a business by offering expanded trade credit to business customers and suggests a number of alternatives for funding that expanded trade credit.

An obvious question is "Which funding alternative should I pursue?" My recommendation for pursing the alternatives are listed below. This recommendation ranks the alternatives, with the less costly listed above the more costly. It also turns out that the less costly alternatives, if they are available, are generally better for the trade credit seller in terms of the value delivered, in addition to being less expensive. However, the dilemma is that the less costly (and better) alternative may simply not be available for a particular industry or in a particular market.

References to these sources are provided in Appendix B.

ALTERNATIVE 1:

Ask your vendors for longer payment terms (Chapter 9). Having suppliers provide longer payment terms, if you purchase goods or services from suppliers, is the least costly (free) and frequently the easiest source of additional capital. While additional terms from vendors may help supply some of the additional credit required, it may not be enough. In that case, move to Alternative 2.

ALTERNATIVE 2:

Use FTRANS® Trade Credit Express™ to outsource to financial institutions the risk, business processes, and funding of trade credit (Chapter 10). The FTRANS alternative may be available to trade credit sellers in the geographic markets being served by banks

currently working with FTRANS. It also may be available nationwide
for certain trade credit sellers, including venture-backed companies,
law and accounting firms, advertising agencies, trade associations, and
broadcast stations. (Note: as has been pointed out elsewhere in this
book, I founded FTRANS and have an economic stake in its future. I
enthusiastically believe that FTRANS is the best alternative for many
businesses.) If FTRANS trade credit outsourcing is not yet available
for your industry or geographic location, move to Alternative 3.

ALTERNATIVE 3:

Other trade credit outsourcing (Chapter 10). There are other accounts
receivable management companies, such as The CIT Group, that serve
larger companies nationwide in specific core industries. These trade
credit outsourcing solutions offer many of the same advantages as
FTRANS. It is worth checking with them to see if they serve your
industry or size of business. If trade credit outsourcing via Alternative
2 or 3 is not available for you, move to Alternative 4.

ALTERNATIVE 4:

Bank lending (Chapter 9). Ask your bank if they can provide funding
to expand the terms you offer customers. But, be careful – make sure
they really provide funding based on accounts receivable as collateral
before you give then an application. The reason for this caution is not
the cost in dollars of making an application to a bank, but, a cost in
your personal credit score, which is negatively impacted every time a
credit inquiry is made. Press your banker carefully on this topic. Ask
him or her if they make C&I loans based on the assets of the business
or another form of asset-based lending. If they cannot answer
affirmatively, look for another bank. Ask your banker if he or she
knows a bank that does make C&I working capital loans to businesses
like yours. (Bankers generally know what the competition is doing
and most bankers try to be helpful – he or she may tell you if they
know.) Remember, bank lending is just that – it is just a loan, and
does nothing to reduce the risk or administrative burden of granting

trade credit. Yet, it may be your best alternative if FTRANS is not available in your market or CIT does not serve your industry or size of business. Your best bet is always a bank with whom you have some history, but if they are not C&I lenders, you have to look elsewhere – either other banks, or receivables discounting, Alternative 5.

ALTERNATIVE 5:

Receivables discounting (Chapter 9). This alternative is listed below trade credit outsourcing and bank lending because it is generally more expensive than FTRANS, CIT, and other trade credit outsourcing alternatives, or bank financing. It is still just lending, like bank lending, and does not provide for outsourcing of risk and administration, as is the case with trade credit outsourcing. However, it may be the only alternative available. If the profit margins in the business are adequate, using the additional funding available from even receivables financing to grow sales by expanding trade credit to customers can make very good sense. If receivables financing is not available, consider Alternative 6.

ALTERNATIVE 6:

Equity or loans from owner (Chapter 9). This alternative is listed next to last, even lower than receivables discounting, for three reasons. First, Alternatives 1 through 5 may be accessed quickly and economically when compared to the profit opportunity from growing sales. Second, many owners have already invested all they can or should in their business. If you have surplus funds invested elsewhere, you may want to consider the rate that you are earning on those investments as an alternative to bank loans or receivables discounting. However, the third reason is that if you can finance growth with OPM (other peoples money) without giving up ownership in your company, that approach provides you with the most flexibility in the long term. Once you invest money in your company, you may be stuck with that investment for a long period of time – you lose flexibility. If you fail with Alternatives 1 through 6, then move on to Alternative 7.

ALTERNATIVE 7:

Equity from venture investors or equity or loans from friends and family (Chapter 9). This type of financing takes too long, especially if you are trying to fund growth and need to respond to the current market opportunity. With this type of funding, you give up future earnings and you may give up control. My advice is to consider this Alternative 7 as a last resort only.

CONCLUSION

Summary of strategy and benefits for business.

The growth strategy advocated by this book is simple: **give your business customers more credit on longer terms**. This strategy could have two very positive benefits:

- First, for many B2B sellers, it can immediately increase sales.

- Second, it will help develop more enduring relationships with business buyers.

The strategy has several important features:

- It is easy to implement, if you have access to sufficient capital; alternatives for obtaining this capital are covered in Chapters 9 and 10.

- It is inexpensive relative to the potential gains as discussed in Chapter 8.

- The cost is tied to results – you spend money only as sales increase, except for a minor amount to advertise the availability of expanded credit for your customers.

- Using trade credit to grow sales has been a part of commerce for thousands of years and is a rational strategy year after year. But, it is particularly valuable at this time since business buyers face greater constraints on their access to capital.

APPENDIX A: GLOSSARY OF IMPORTANT TERMS

ACCOUNTS

Defined by the Uniform Commercial Code as the right to receive payments (accounts receivable) and the obligation to make payments (accounts payable) that arise from the sale of goods or services.

B2B OR BUSINESS TO BUSINESS

The sale of goods or services by a business to another business. Usually also includes the sales to governments. At about $19 trillion in 2007, B2B transactions make up about 60% of total sales in the United States. See GDP.

FACTOR

Original meaning: the financial institution that purchases **accounts** from a **trade credit seller** (without recourse). Newer meaning: a financial institution that makes a loan to a **trade credit seller** and has a lien on the **accounts** as collateral. (As discussed at length in Chapter 9, I view these two definitions as contradictory.)

GDP OR GROSS DOMESTIC PRODUCT

The federal Bureau of Economic Analysis describers GDP as "the value of goods and services produced by the U.S. economy in a given period of time." BEA reports that GDP in the U.S. at the end of 2007 was $13.5 trillion. GDP counts only the final value of the good or services, not the intermediary prices charged by a business seller to the next business buyer in the supply chain, which intermediate sale was likely made with trade credit. Each of the intermediate sales is counted when considering total trade credit sales. The total intermediate sales were about $19 trillion in 2007, about 1.5 times the amount of GDP.

TRADE CREDIT

The Federal Reserve Board definition is: "**Trade credit** and **trade debt** are accounts receivable and payable arising from the sale of business-related goods and services." [emphasis added]. **Trade credit** transactions were about $19 trillion in the United States in 2007, nearly 50% larger than the $13 trillion of consumer credit transactions. More than 97% of trade credit transactions in the U.S. are made in the traditional way of the seller extending trade credit to the buyer; less than 3% of trade credit sales are made through credit cards.

APPENDIX B: SOURCES OF ADDITIONAL INFORMATION

Sources of Capital

FTRANS

The creator of **Trade Credit Express**™ that allows trade credit sellers to outsource much of the risk, business processes, and funding of operating a trade credit system (patent pending). Not available yet in all states for all B2B sellers.

www.ftrans.net
T: (678) 268-4033

THE CIT GROUP / COMMERCIAL SERVICES

The nation's largest true factor.
www.cit.com
T: (704) 339-2928

COMMERCIAL FINANCE ASSOCIATION

CFA is the trade association of true factors and asset-based lenders. Online directory of lenders available.
www.cfa.com

INTERNATIONAL FACTORING ASSOCIATION

Despite its name, IFA is really an association for receivables discounting, not true factoring. But, it does have an online directory of those lenders.
www.factoring.org

APPENDIX C: FINANCIAL MODELS USED FOR ANALYSIS AND EXPLANATION

CAPITAL FLOW MODEL

The Capital Flow Model (CFM) was developed by the author to enhance comprehension of the flows of capital in and out of the enterprise – the "sources and uses". CFM is a presentation of Symbolic Accounting ™, which is based on principals of systems engineering and analysis that define and measure inputs and outputs of systems. CFM uses information from traditional financial statements to present in a graphical form the critical inputs and outputs of capital. CFM adheres to the traditional algebra of the balance sheet in which Assets = Liabilities + Equity, but characterizes Liabilities and Equity as "Sources," or inputs, and Assets (except Cash) as "Uses," or outputs. Cash is the resulting capital "in the box". (A patent application has been filed on Symbolic Accounting and covers CFM.)

The advantage of CFM, as discussed in Chapter 3, is that it enables rapid comprehension of the balance sheet and flow of capital in an enterprise or an industry in terms of Sources, Uses, and resulting Cash. It also enables easy comparison between:

- Individual businesses (see the comparison between Wal-Mart and IBM in Chapter 3)

- An industry and an individual enterprise

- Industries

- Groups of industries (such as retail and wholesale)

- Industries grouped in geographic areas

Financial Models and Data Sources

For an interesting interactive view of the Capital Flow Model, visit www.ftrans.net/cfm.

THE THREE CS OF LENDING

The Three Cs of Lending (Capacity, Collateral, and Character), which is used throughout this book, has been the core component of credit training for bankers for many years. See Chapter 5 for a detailed explanation of the use of the Three Cs in specific lending situations. For additional discussion on this topic, type "Three Cs of Lending" in the Google search engine.

Printed in the United States
202759BV00002B/223-924/P

9 780972 794213